The Peppered
By Adam Pr

To Dad

Thanks to Melissa Viney, Richard Burrell, Mark Hennessy, Billy Brannigan, Carol Cooper, Elizabeth Reed, Paul Ricketts and Henry Kinross

It was a dreary Friday morning and Michael Peel awoke and lay listening to the rain pattering on the window in his comfortable, tatty bedroom. For a while he stared sightlessly at an old pair of pale blue espadrilles in a string bag that hung on the back of the door as his wife of the last forty-two years brushed her teeth in the bathroom. Michael used the few moments of waking repose to order his thoughts.

Once a year, Michael Peel and Associates undertook a small but nevertheless important public relations service for a personal loan company, a direct ancestor of the payday loan firms of today. The task was not onerous, involving little more than the now archaic business of sending a few faxes to the press as well as the organisation of a board meeting and a lunch, but there were opportunities for cock ups and anxiety is sometimes generated, not by the difficulty of a task, but by the level of importance attached to its being carried off without a hitch. In addition, Michael Peel and Associates only really had one employee, which was of course himself.

He had selected salmon for the lunch, on the principal that he liked it, but a vague memory of someone saying something negative about fish caused him to roll over and swing his legs off the edge of the bed, the whole movement powered by an adrenalin rush. Charles Dryesdale, the CEO of the personal loan firm Dryesdale Ltd., had once told him he was sick of salmon. Why was he only remembering this now? His ageing brain was letting him down.

He heard the toilet flush and the sound of taps running and he relaxed slightly. Caroline would reassure him. There was a sharp *clack* as the bathroom door opened and he heard her bare feet approaching across the upstairs landing. He remained seated on the edge of the bed as she pushed open the bedroom door, still rubbing moisturiser into her face, her dyed ash-blonde hair in disarray.

"There's a problem with fish," he said, enjoying the cryptic nature of this short sentence. Good to keep the old girl on her toes, he thought, expecting a note of ritual irritation in her reply.

Instead she let out an abrupt bark of naked terror.

It was not a sound Mr Peel had heard before but he interpreted it as meaning that an intruder was in the room behind him. He instinctively raised his hands to protect the back of his head before turning and scanning the bedroom for assailants.

The lack of an intruder confused him. He looked up towards the ceiling as though expecting to find some fiendish Ninja figure affixed to the picture rail. Finding nothing, he turned back to Caroline for her explanation, only to find that she had reversed out of the bedroom and was standing with her back pressed to the wall of the upstairs landing.

"What's happening?" he demanded with real urgency.

"Michael?" she shouted.

"What are yo..?"

"Michael?" she shouted again, her questioning inflection making no sense whatsoever.

"What are you doing woman?" he demanded, beginning to give rein to his mounting irritation. "Why are you shouting my bloody name when I'm sitting here in front of you?"

He stood up and she glanced at him with fresh alarm. She seemed to find him abhorrent.

"Get out of my bedroom at once," she commanded. The order was strident and delivered at a low pitch, similar to that used to rebuke Robert, their spaniel, when he shat on the carpet.

"What the hell has got into you?" asked Mr Peel, but instead of answering she slid silently away down the corridor, knocking, with her head, a series of framed prints featuring the moths of Papua New Guinea. One of these fell to the ground, its glass front shattering, but she didn't even glance at it. She gripped the top of the banister and deftly swung herself around it, so that she was immediately heading, still barefoot and in her pale green cotton nightdress, down the stairs.

Mr Peel was extremely annoyed and he seriously considered shouting the word "bugger" with all the force of his lungs but held off out of a desire to get things on an even keel. It was a very important day and his wife's alarming behaviour was threatening everything. His mind raced through the details of their financial woes.

Unlike most of their friends, Mr and Mrs Peel were still saddled with large mortgage payments. As a Lloyd's 'Name' of long standing, Mr Peel had benefited from hefty dividends right up to the end of the 1980's, when he had abruptly discovered the true meaning of the words 'unlimited liability'. Members were required to cover massive losses and many went bankrupt, but Mr Peel saw it as a matter of honour to meet his obligations. He had sold what he owned and started again.

His recovery from this catastrophe had been hobbled by the recession of the early 1990's, which had cruelly depleted his business, forcing him to sell what remained of his share portfolio, the value of which was at a pitifully low ebb, just to keep up with the mortgage payments. Now, in the mid nineties, although the economy had recovered, Mr Peel's old clients tended to see him as someone approaching retirement (as indeed he was) and they took their business elsewhere. Bills seemed to come in at murderous rate every day and there had been occasions when he had been forced to ask Caroline to cut back on the weekly groceries. They were due to make a mortgage payment the following week and he needed to deposit the £12,000 that was due from Dryesdale or the final series of direct debit payments simply would not occur. Until his Royal Sun Alliance pension kicked in the following spring this was the last lump of money he was likely to receive.

He organised the harsh facts in his mind, preparing a short and serious speech that he would deliver to Caroline in the kitchen. Whatever nonsense she had rustled up, she was to lay it aside. The truth was they were sunk without the £12,000 and she would be made to calm down and put her hysterics off until tomorrow.

He walked into the bathroom and as he did he heard his wife talking on the telephone in the kitchen below. She sounded calmer, as though dealing with an urgent plumbing problem. He could not hear what she was saying but the sound reassured him. When all was said and done she was a practical old boot. Perhaps she was checking herself into an asylum.

The bathroom door was open and he stepped up to the sink, looking down at the chaotic arrangement of toothbrushes and disposable razors in an old chipped Fortnum and Mason mug. He homed in on his blue toothbrush and was about to pluck it out when he became aware of a shadow in the mirror. It was inappropriately dark and caused a pure abstract terror to grip his heart. He looked up and found himself staring, eyeball-to-eyeball, at what he could only describe as a black man.

In the first moment of shock his mind functioned clumsily – making false, childlike assumptions that bore not the faintest whisper of logic. In short he concluded that, during the night, someone must have applied a blowtorch to his head. The obvious corollary to this, that had they done so he would have known something about it, followed on with great rapidity. The next thought was that he was extremely, dangerously ill. He had been attacked by a plague that had brutally interfered with his complexion and his hair. But by now an entirely different level of observation had kicked in and he was starting to digest an even more outlandish and terrifying truth.

He stood rigid with terror – looking into the face in the mirror – searching it for some sign of Michael Peel. But it was not Michael Peel. It was a stranger.

A black stranger, apparently a good ten years younger than himself and, far from being burnt or plague ridden, in apparent good health.

He stepped aside so he could stop having to look at the wide-eyed impostor. Instantly the harshest, whitest heat of the terror just cooled sufficiently for him to be able to take a breath. He looked at the palms of his hands – they were darker than his normal tone, but not as dark as the face he had just seen. For a moment he wondered if his mind had played a trick – exaggerating the seriousness of the situation – but then he turned the hands over. The skin was an even rich brown colour. He ripped at the front of his cotton pyjama top and the small white buttons pinged about the room. His chest, too, was the smooth dark colour of roasted coffee beans.

"What the buggery is happening?" he shouted.

He looked once more in the mirror – this time staring into his own eyeballs. It was a strangely reassuring thing to do because at last he recognized himself – the man inside. He was still Michael Peel – something had just happened to his outside.

"Caroline!" he bellowed – then paused – fighting frantically to get a hold of himself. He had to take control, to bring some order and reason to the state of affairs. He was still Michael Peel – and that counted for a great deal. This was simply a freakish medical situation and the starting point would be to call Dr Singh at the Farley Medical Centre.

He found Caroline standing turned away from him by the kitchen table holding the telephone to her ear. Robert the spaniel stared up at her, his tail waving uncertainly. Usually he would be wolfing down his breakfast from his tin bowl and Classic FM would be playing. None of this was happening and the dog, a naturally nervous and conservative creature, was anxious.

"He's still in the house," Caroline was saying into the telephone, "yes… no I haven't seen my husband all morning – I've already said that twice. Could you please just...". Mr Peel calmly took the phone from her hand – causing her to produce, for the first time, a proper scream.

"For God's sake Caroline, will you calm down," he said. She was trapped, now, in a tiny cul-de-sac created by the kitchen table, the Rayburn cooker, the sink, and the black stranger holding the telephone in his hand.

"The police will be here any minute," she said, regaining her spirit of pure Home Counties grit. "I suggest you get out of this house at once."

"We don't need the police," he replied, calmly but firmly, and he put the phone to his ear.

"This is Mr Peel speaking – I am Caroline Peel's husband and everything is alright – there's just been a misunderstanding because I have developed an alarming rash in the night. I am going to seek medical assistance."

There was a prolonged silence at the other end of the line. At last a woman with a flat Estuary accent spoke.

"Right – did you say you are Mr Peel, the husband of the lady who I was just speaking with just now?"

"Yes I did," he replied, impressed by his own patience.

"And are you saying that you require an ambulance Mr Peel?"

"An ambulance? No – no I'm going to see the family doctor. It's just a very serious rash."

"Would you be able to kindly put your wife back on the line so that she can confirm your statement that you are saying to me – would that be alright for you to do that for me now sir?"

He felt a wave of irritation – both at her awful syntax and the fact that a man couldn't be trusted to speak for his own wife.

"Yes of course – I'll put her on."

Caroline eyed the phone as he covered the receiver so the operator wouldn't hear.

"Look Caroline, would you please calm down, I'm not a black man, I'm me – it's me – Michael. I don't know what's happened but we don't need the police - that's just going to bugger up the whole day."

He held the phone out to her. As she took it she seemed sadly resigned, as though a great plan had collapsed about her ears. She spoke to the operator while Mr Peel stood, unknowingly blocking her escape, with his arms folded.

"Hello this is Caroline Peel,' she said. There was a pause as the operator spoke to her. She replied unnaturally, as though reading lines from a play. "Yes – everything he said is true…a rash yes…yes that would be good – thank you. I have to hang up now."

She handed the telephone back to him and Mr Peel took it over to a display case full of British moths that he had collected as a young man. On top of it sat a worn phone book.

As he searched through for Dr Singh's number, Caroline flitted out through the kitchen door and he saw her flash past the window with the dog trailing after her, his tail wagging excitedly at the prospect of an unscheduled walkies.

"Where are you going woman?" Mr Peel shouted. "You're going to catch a filthy bloody cold."

His hand shook as he tried to flip open the 'd' for doctor and he managed to drop the book on the floor, prompting an explosive shout of "Bugger!" Finally he had the number and, after an infuriating wait, he got through to the reception of the surgery in Farley.

"Hello – good morning," he said, realising, for the first time, that his voice was very much his own. This filled him with a sudden sense of power.

"This is Michael Peel from Orchard House – I need an emergency appointment right away please."

****

As Mr Peel did a three-point turn in the driveway he reversed the Rover into a sit-on toy tractor belonging to his grandchild. The grunting sound as it fragmented beneath the rear bumper forced him to take stock. He was now wearing his best dark blue chalk-stripe suit but he was still a black man and he was running late. In the Royal Marines, in which he had done service for six years from 1966, they had been taught that the more drastic the situation, the calmer you needed to be. In a crisis the first thing that happens is fools panic, mistakes are made, technology fails and men injure themselves and not the enemy.

"I'm doing what any sensible man would do – I'm getting medical help – everything is in hand and I just need to calm down and proceed cautiously," he reflected.

He negotiated the car carefully out of the entrance to Orchard House, where he paused while a car raced past. He turned left and immediately saw Caroline up ahead, gripping Robert by the collar and waving frantically at a car coming the other way.

So many aspects of the sight were deeply unsettling – the fact that she was barefooted, in her night dress, in the rain, on the hazardous road with the dog not on a lead – that Mr Peel had to partially shut the situation out of his consciousness.

A car approaching Caroline from the other direction slowed as the driver peered at the alarming vision. He performed mental gymnastics to persuade himself that it was not his business to stop for elderly women with dementia and dogs. He drove on, giving her a wide berth.

Mr Peel slowed to a stop beside his wife and opened the window. She looked at him with great sorrow. It was as though her entire understanding of the essential goodness and safety of her life had been annihilated in the time it takes to boil an egg.

"Caroline will you please just listen to me for a moment before you get yourself killed."

The word 'killed' acted like a cattle prod applied between her shoulder blades. She flinched violently, released the dog and started walking briskly away along the side of the road. He crept along beside her in the car – employing all his will to speak calmly.

"I am me - this is me – Michael – I've turned into a black man in the night." The desire to see the look on a man's face when he said something so extravagantly insane got the better of her and she glanced once at him briefly. "Look – alright." His mind raced as he searched for personal information – something only she and he would know.

"Three months ago I had an operation. It was on my arsehole – a fistula – there – now why would a strange black man know that?"

To his astonishment she started screaming for help. It was such a grossly unhelpful thing for her to do that he felt a gush of blood run to his head. When a car horn then beeped behind him – a long, impudent beep – this rush of blood immediately precipitated a storm of fury, which had him grasping at his door handle.

He turned in a rage to the car behind and began to stride towards it. It was a smart black Range Rover with a bullish looking white man in his thirties at the wheel – but he seemed to shrink visibly at the sight of Mr Peel approaching. His hands made desperate apology signs as though Mr Peel were a terrifying ogre but it was the cold rain falling on Mr Peel's head that brought him to his senses. Road rage was not going to help his situation. He got back into the car, vaguely wondering why the man had looked quite so terrified, and expended some of his anger by gunning the accelerator, so that he passed his wife at speed.

"I'm just making the situation worse," he reasoned – at which point he became aware of the siren and flashing lights of a police car, turning off the main road and into the lane. As it shot passed him he felt momentarily reassured. They would at least get Caroline and the dog off the road and back into the house.

At the doctor's surgery he approached the familiar reception with the confidence of someone who had been there many times – but the two middle-aged ladies who ran the reception looked up at him with synchronised alarm. The more officious-looking of the two, with her spectacles perched half-way down her nose, was in the middle of talking on the telephone but stopped mid-sentence to look at him and seemed to inflate her lungs as though getting ready for strenuous exercise. He had intended to state his own name but their startled eyes quickly persuaded him that getting past these formidable gatekeepers was going to require a certain amount of cunning.

"Good morning. I rang earlier – sorry, I mean Michael Peel rang earlier."

"Yes?" said the woman, who still held the telephone in her hand. Her tone suggested that the fact that Michael Peel had telephoned was completely irrelevant.

"Michael is a very good friend of mine and – this is terribly embarrassing…" He trailed off, hoping this would be sufficient.

"We're beyond embarrassment here," said the woman, "did you want to make an appointment for yourself?"

"Yes I do," he said, "an emergency appointment."

"There isn't any such thing as an emergency appointment I'm afraid - that's a bit of a myth." She reached for a form and a pen. "But you can wait – would you please fill out a temporary patient form?"

Mr Peel had a vision of himself hunched over some tortuous form, having to make up names and addresses for a black man who did not exist. "But didn't you make an emergency appointment for Michael Peel about fifteen minutes ago?" he asked – being careful to suggest, by his tone, a genuine question rather than some sort of rebuke. This silenced the woman. It was only a momentary silence but for her this was clearly a near defeat. Mr Peel pressed his advantage.

"Michael Peel actually made the appointment for me. He knew that you'd only stretch the rules for him because he's been coming for years – and he banked on you having the goodness to see his friend right away because of the seriousness of my condition."

She reached for the right words to bat away these specious arguments and he sensed that he had only a microsecond. He brought out the big guns.

"Michael would have driven me here but – his wife has suffered a turn."

"Caroline? What sort of turn?" she asked, genuinely concerned.

"It's alright - an ambulance has been called and – look it's been quite a morning and I really…"

"Can you just wait a moment?" she interrupted and wordlessly handed the telephone to her associate – who had sat frozen throughout, as though witnessing a brawl in a pub.

"Come in and take a seat please," said Dr Singh. He was tapping something into his computer and he glanced very briefly at Mr Peel as he sat down.

"Usually for a new patient we take your details outside but on this occasion I don't mind putting them straight into the computer."

"Well I am very grateful to you for seeing me at such short notice," said Mr Peel, feeling, as he settled into the chair, a growing sense of calm and wellbeing. He had managed to get himself in front of a man of science, a man who would be fascinated by his remarkable condition. It occurred to him that Dr Singh had an opportunity here – he might be the first to identify a new syndrome. He might get an article in The Lancet.

"May I please take your name?" said Dr Singh.

"Well actually Doctor – I am…" Mr Peel hesitated before taking the plunge. "Can you bear with me for a moment and take it on my word that I am Michael Peel?"

Dr Singh's eyes momentarily darted at his patient, but the sight of the tall distinguished black man with greying temples, sitting casually with his legs crossed, as though he owned the surgery, reassured him.

"Michael Peel?" he replied calmly, and with a twinkle of sudden humour in his eyes. "This is quite some coincidence because we have a Michael Peel already on our books here."

"I am that self-same Michael Peel," replied Mr Peel, "and difficult as that may be for you to accept – I would ask that you do accept it now as a statement of fact. Something extraordinary has happened to me in the night and my first thought was to come here and show the problem to you – I feel that you are one of the few people I can rely on to be sensible about it. "

Dr Singh had of course dealt with mental illness in his time and he did not necessarily feel out of his depth, but something about the calm assurance of this man and the way it was so deeply out of sync with the extremity of his delusion made him nervous. He decided to humour him.

"Well - of course if you say you are - as you put it – that self-same Michael Peel, I certainly don't want to argue with you. So what, if I might ask this self-same Mr Peel, seems to be the trouble?"

The question struck Mr Peel as a real step backwards.

"What," continued Dr Singh, filling Mr Peel's silence, "can I help you with today?"

"Help me with? I want you to help me – I want you to tell me why I have turned into a black man and help me turn back into a white man." Mr Peel was struggling not to swear.

"Help you turn back into a white man?"

"Yes – as you can see quite clearly – I have turned into a black man – it happened in the night. It has given my wife a terrible fright and my first thought was to come here and speak with a man of intelligence and reason who can give me the diagnosis and treatment I need. Is there – I mean is there any precedence for this sort of thing? Is this a recognised condition?"

Dr Singh struggled with mixed feelings. The mention of the alarm of Mrs Peel was clearly a serious turn of events. Rosemary at the desk had mentioned something about her having a turn. This man had quite possibly been to the Peel family home where God only knew what lunacy had been perpetrated. Clearly he needed to get the police involved but there was another aspect to all of this. What this man was saying was fundamentally offensive to him and, perhaps against his better judgement, he felt the need to take a stand.

" Mr...Mr Peel, I do not know if you have noticed but I am myself a man of - of colour."

"Of course," replied Mr Peel, a sense of unease creeping rapidly upon him.

"So you will, I am sure, forgive me for pointing out that - being a man of colour is not, certainly the last time I checked, a medical condition."

"Well no of course not – I mean that's not..."

"In fact I think we can say with some confidence that it is not a matter for a doctor or indeed a matter requiring any kind of medical intervention."

"But my point is that I am a white man," said Mr Peel with sudden urgency.

"I beg to disagree," Dr Singh replied, making the sort of moves now that a man makes when he is about to leave a room.

"I was a white man and I have turned into a black man – it's like that pop star – what's his name Jackson something – the one who turned white."

"Will you excuse me for one moment?"

"Look – can you please not leave?" pleaded Mr Peel, recognising the nervous, jerky manner of a person about to call the emergency services. "I really am in the most terrible dire straits here. I am not imputing that…"

"Please Mr Peel – just sit quietly there…"

"I will not sit quietly. I am in the most awful bloody situation!"

Dr Singh was now standing at the open door and Mr Peel's raised voice had alerted not only the receptionists but the small group of patients in the waiting room who, though they continued to stare at old Hello and OK magazines, were both terrified and thrilled at the mounting uproar.

"Look," said Mr Peel, bringing out what he believed was his ace card, "I know all my medical history – ask me any question."

"Please Mr Peel, just wait there, I will be back in one tiny half minute." He nodded imperceptibly at Rosemary, who immediately understood that the police were needed and began to act accordingly.

"I had a fistula on my ars… on my rectum – just recently – you arranged the operation. An inch-long fistula."

This horrendous information, almost bellowed, caused a shift in mood in the waiting room where every last person could not resist peering openly at the angry black man who was now standing in the corridor shouting about his bottom. The sight of all these people looking at him as he revealed this intimate information sent him into an instant rage.

"Do you think I enjoy yelling about anal fistulas? It's the second time today I've had to try and wake up the feeble-minded to the reality of this monstrous situation and I am getting mighty fed up with it. I have turned into a black man and I need help. Is there anyone here who is not a hair-trigger hysteric who can give me some medical fucking help?"

****

As he drove away towards Tonbridge another police car flashed past in the drizzle and Mr Peel momentarily imagined the unfamiliar excitement that must be spreading through the local constabulary. A black man gone berserk, a respectable middle-aged white businessman missing, his car stolen, his wife no doubt shocked to the marrow and now probably wrapped in a blanket, sipping tea while some policewoman, trained to the gills in treating post-traumatic stress disorder, comforted her with practiced sincerity. A wave of self-pity washed over Mr Peel and he felt like a child again. A child who was in terrible trouble for something he had not done.

But it was not a day for self-pity. In an hour the annual results of Dryesdale Ltd. would come through by fax. The figures would have to be retyped onto Michael Peel and Associates headed paper and then faxed through to the financial press. It was a fiddly business, which stretched his little office to its limits and invariably involved technical breakdown and swearing. One year he had been forced to ask the next door office to let him use their fax machine and he had been astonished to find it entirely peopled by wiry little Japanese men in dark suits. They had milked the situation pitilessly – leaving him with the impression that they were taking long-delayed revenge for their nation's defeat in the Second World War.

The typing and faxing, the board meeting and lunch – all these things would need to start happening soon and Mr Peel keenly felt the need to take command. As he entered the outskirts of Tonbridge he passed a red telephone box and, seeing an inviting expanse of empty parking places beyond it, he spontaneously pulled in and parked. But instead of getting out of the car he paused. There was no point in calling the office until he had figured out what to say.

Michael Peel and Associates was run out of a small office five floors up in an ageing 1970s oblong block on the fringes of the City of London. Mr Peel did not actually have formal associates but shared the office with two other men with whom he had a complex symbiotic working relationship.

The idea of telling his two colleagues that he had turned into a black man was simply unthinkable – they would just assume he was mucking about and berate him for oversleeping on such an important day. Should he go to the office at all? Could he instead call in sick and ask Nigel to handle the board meeting and the lunch? The thought made him wince.

The problem with sending Nigel along to handle the day's events was that he was 'not quite the full shilling' as his other colleague, Sackville, had once put it. Nigel had attended some school in Chelmsford that had bequeathed him an accent that summonsed a dreary wet Tuesday morning in suburbia. If there was one thing you could say with absolute certainty about Charles Dryesdale, the CEO of Dryesdale Ltd, it was that he was an appalling snob. Unleashing Nigel's nasal drone into his board meeting and lunch would be about as tactful as giving vent to a colossal fart.

He wondered if perhaps he could ask Sackville to do it – and the thought gave him such a fright that his mouth involuntarily dropped open.

Briar Sackville was rotund, amusing, prickly, charming and infinitely arrogant - an immaculately tailored hive of contradictions. Could he really call him up and ask him to take over the proceedings for the day? Sackville was capable of glad-handing, of making well-judged small talk and introducing proceedings with a witty speech. But as for what might be termed actual work – the idea of depending on him conjured a vision of a fat man getting into a muddle, sweat glistening on his wide brow and a mini-avalanche of press releases fluttering to the ground.

The next thought, which seemed so perfect it caused his pulse to race momentarily, was that Sackville and Nigel could form a team – with Nigel quietly rushing around with press releases and bottles of water and Sackville simply gliding about lending his old Etonian charm to proceedings. But the dream collapsed as quickly as it had materialised when the face of Charles Drysedale loomed up in his imagination, weary and pained with disappointment. "Just one day a year Michael," he could almost hear him saying, "I ask you to earn your fee – and you've let me down – were you really so ill that you couldn't struggle into London? I really think we should adjust your remuneration downwards. " Seen in this light, the dream of calling in sick was nothing but a cruel mirage. What is more, it occurred to Mr Peel that neither Sackville nor Nigel had sufficient knowledge of the various personalities on the board of Drysedale Ltd. The seething internal politics of this body of men had to be carefully corralled, calling on what Mr Peel possessed in the way of diplomatic skills and putting him under such strain that he was usually left with the sense that he had really earned his annual fee of £12,000.

This left him with the awkward and stubborn fact that he was (and he briefly checked in the car's mirror in case the situation had changed) a black man. One thing was certain – if he entered the office claiming to be Michael Peel the hysteria he had so far witnessed would only be repeated, with flamboyant variations courtesy of Nigel and Sackville. In fact, it was highly unlikely that he would even be able to get past the security man who sat, pole axed with boredom, making life difficult for the occasional deliveryman. "I still have my voice," thought Mr Peel, and a plan quickly formed that would at least allow him to buy some time.

"Hello, how can I help?" chirped the voice of Nigel on the heavy black handset in the telephone booth, with its usual metallic smell of urine and cold steel. There had been endless arguments about how the telephone should be answered at the office and they had been forced to settle on this rather bland solution, which avoided giving undue prominence to any one of their enterprises.

"Nigel, it's Michael."

"Good God – Michael – where the fuck are you? Isn't today the big day for Bleed 'em Dryesdale ?"

"Look I've had the most God awful morning – Caroline's gone mad."

"What have you done to her you old bastard?"

"Nigel – this is serious – she's really lost her mind. We've had to call in the police and everything."

"The police? Oh I see – you mean she's really…"

"I mean she's raving. It's no joke I can assure you. Look I need your help to get through today. It's all hands to the pumps."

"Yes of course."

"Have the figures come through?"

"Not yet."

"When they do can you make a start – typing them up and all that?"

"Of course – don't worry Michael – I've got it all in hand – I can do the board meeting and lunch too if you like – just give me a few pointers."

"It's alright, I'm sending an old friend."

"What do you mean an old friend?"

"He's someone I was at school with - he's a good chap."

"But surely he won't know anything."

"He's been staying with us – I've - I've fully briefed him on everything."

"Really?" said Nigel, his voice filled with doubt.

"He's in PR himself and he's taken a great interest in everything I've been doing."

"How very peculiar."

"Nigel, this is an emergency situation so could we possibly keep the banter down to the bare minimum?"

"Right you are – what's this man's name – I'll have to tell reception."

Mr Peel felt himself lurch towards a precipice. It had not occurred to him to make up a name for the black incarnation of himself. He reached desperately for a black person whose name he could appropriate.

The truth was he did not have a single black friend or acquaintance. This was not a fact he had ever had to confront before but he now confronted it head on – and then quickly swerved off into trying to think of famous black people. The first person that came into his head was Lenny Henry the comedian, who he had seen the night before in comedy drama about a chef – but neither part of this name seemed particularly plausible. There was Nelson Mandela, of course – could he be Nelson Henry? It didn't sound right at all.

"Hello?" said Nigel into the growing silence.

Lenny Mandela was clearly hopeless. Who was that American actor? Sydney Poitier – he couldn't be Poitier, it sounded too French – and Sydney Henry was blatantly ridiculous. Sydney Mandela likewise.

"Michael are you there?" asked Nigel – a note of suspicion creeping into his voice. "Can you just tell me his name?"

"Yes he's called…" It was hopeless – he would just have to take the plunge. He'd have to make something up from scratch. He thought of Africa. The film Zulu. Mud huts. Starving children, swollen tummies. Could he be a chief? Chief something – Buthelezi? Bantu? He was about to say the word 'chief' when he imagined Nigel calling Charles Dryesdale to tell him that the Chief of the Bantu people would be representing Michael Peel and Associates at the board meeting. Clearly that would be the end of everything. He needed to be an English black man. Weren't they often called Winston? But that was in the sixties. Things had moved on.

"Michael are you still there?" asked Nigel.

"Yes – his name's – his name's Henry – Henry Espadrille."

"I beg your pardon?"

"Henry Espadrille – now listen he's a black man." The word Espadrille had popped into his head from nowhere. It was a ridiculous word to seize on – but by God he was going to stick by it now.

"A black man called Henry Espadrille? Are you taking the piss?"

"Nigel, I am telling you that is the man's name and he's on his way to the office now."

"But it doesn't sound real."

"Well you're going to bloody well find out that it is real soon enough. And I'd be grateful if you'd take a day off from being an appalling racist if that's not too much trouble, and give the man a helping hand."

"I'm not a racist," said Nigel, clearly hurt, "I've got more friends of colour than you have."

"The fact that you're on first-name terms with an Indian newsagent does not cancel out the fact that you are a dyed-in-the-wool Essex racist of the old school. Look, I don't want to get into this now – can you just please be civil to Henry…"

"Espadrille."

"That's right - and if it's not too demeaning for you I would be eternally grateful if you could regard him as working entirely with my authority."

"You mean I'm supposed to take orders from him," said Nigel.

"That's exactly what I mean, Nigel." And with that he hung up.

****

On the train to London, Mr Peel read The Telegraph and ate a sausage sandwich to reassure himself with the totems of normality. At Hildenborough station, just as he had started the crossword, an acquaintance of his boarded the train. A raucous aristocratic blonde in her late forties, she clattered noisily into the carriage, spilling coffee on her hand and cursing with the infinite arrogance of the high-bred and attractive.

For some time Mr Peel had been exchanging a daily and increasingly daring banter with this woman, whom he had once met at a local drinks party. She had recently taken to removing invisible fluff from his shoulder and referring to the silver curls at the nape of his neck as 'a bit tasty'. He was no more likely to take this harmless flirtation to the next level than he was going to join the Foreign Legion but it certainly livened up the 8.39 to Charing Cross.

Today, however, they were on the 9.36, and everything about her demeanour suggested she was hungover and running late.

"Put more tonic with it," he commented openly as she tottered past him, forgetting that he was not Mr Peel as she knew him. Startled, she gave him a brief surprised glance then hurried away down the carriage. Mr Peel realised his mistake as soon as the words had left his mouth. He was beginning to form an apology, something about mistaking her for someone else, when she vanished through the connecting doorway. He settled back into his crossword, relieved that the little incident was over. The next clue was, *"Short sub Saharan mix up over old wine (5)"*. Old wine meant "bin end" – he felt that flurry of excitement in the shoulders that heralded the imminent arrival of the answer, but then the blond popped her head back into the carriage from the connecting doorway.

"Fucking impertinence!" She growled in a cigarette-desiccated voice, before vanishing again. A businessman sitting opposite Mr Peel burst out laughing, his eyes inviting him to be best friends in a partnership based on their mutual dislike of such women. But at this point Mr Peel was so close to solving the clue that a troop of nude showgirls could not have distracted him. "One short" meant you took a letter out and "mix up" meant it was an anagram. Bin end – take away the 'd', stir it up, African country - *et voilà* – it was Benin.

He arrived at the office at exactly the same time as Sackville, who occasionally arrived mid-morning if there were matters pending at the little estate in Hampshire. In fact there was an awkward moment as the two men arrived simultaneously at the revolving glass door. Sackville stepped first into the little triangle of space but he caught sight of the familiar chalk stripe suit of the black man behind him. He was so struck by the fact that the man had the exact same suit as his friend and colleague Michael Peel that he turned pointedly, while pushing the revolving door, and stared at him.

Mr Peel returned his brief gaze with a nod and a warm smile – immediately flinging Sackville into a state of embarrassed confusion. Realising his mistake, Mr Peel was careful not to look at him again as he approached the reception but the two men then found themselves standing in the same lift – where Sackville stood facing the wall and planning to take the piss remorselessly out of Mr Peel as soon as he saw him for having a black doppelganger. Mr Peel, however, felt that the situation demanded that he speak. Otherwise, on arrival at the fifth floor, they were going to be in the ludicrous situation of walking together in silence to the same door.

"I think I know your colleague – Michael Peel," he said, startling Sackville and rendering him speechless. "We were at school together". These words served up a whole world of reassurance to Sackville who relaxed visibly.

"You were at St. Paul's with Michael? Same year?" he asked.

"Yes same year – same house actually," replied Michael, realising that there was no limit to how close an acquaintanceship he could claim. He held out his hand and Sackville shook it with guarded warmth.

"Henry Espadrille," said Mr Peel and he went on quickly in the hope that he could blow some smoke over this ridiculous name. "Actually I've come in to help out. Michael's got a spot of trouble – Caroline's had a bit of an episode." Sackville's face transformed into an authentic portrait of concern. If there was one thing that brought out the best in him it was a situation requiring chivalry towards the fairer sex.

"Good heaven's is she alright?" he asked. "What's happened to the old girl?"

"She's had a turn – a sort of episode of – well the truth is - madness."

"Madness?" replied Sackville, unable to disguise a slight shudder of delight at the sheer theatricality of the word. At this point the lift arrived and they began to walk together down the corridor.

"Michael has taken her to hospital where they are checking her out – he's asked me to come in and deputise for him."

Sackville's little eyes swivelled briefly across to look at the black man striding, it seemed to him, with unwarranted confidence down the corridor. He was hurt. In his hour of need Michael had chosen not to call on him, Briar Sackville, who had practically invented public relations, but had preferred to haul in an old coloured schoolmate who made the gauche mistake of exactly copying his old friend's chalk-stripe suit.

However, he was determined to be courteous, if nothing else to demonstrate that he was utterly without prejudice when it came to persons of other races. What is more he was anticipating, with some pleasure, the look on Nigel's face when he saw a black man enter the office as a working colleague who arguably wielded authority over him.

Nigel, however, had had plenty of time to prepare his face for the arrival of Henry Espadrille and he greeted him with an understated friendliness that left Sackville wondering if his own tone had perhaps been somewhat patronising. The figures from Dryesdale Ltd. had come through on the fax machine and Nigel was busily retyping them so they could be printed out on Michael Peel and Associates headed notepaper and faxed on to the press.

The telephone rang and, much to the surprise of his two peers, Mr Peel moved swiftly to answer it, sensing that the slow-moving intellects of the Tonbridge police might have finally cottoned on to the fact that his work place was worth a routine telephone inquiry. His hunch proved to be spot on and he was able to deftly explain to the female constable that Mr Peel "had not yet come in to the office but was expected at any minute." When Sackville looked questioningly at him he covered the receiver and said "bloody photocopier salesman", thus reassuring Sackville and Nigel that he was merely batting away a familiar irritant.

When the telephone rang again Nigel's hand moved like a serpent and he had answered it before Mr Peel had even begun to move. The man making the call was Charles Dryesdale, the CEO of Dryesdale Ltd, and he had had a tiresome morning.

He had wanted to travel from Leycotes, his country estate in Suffolk, the night before but Clotilde, his French wife (a compact and avaricious ex-air hostess from Limoges), had insisted she didn't want to get caught up in Sunday night traffic. This had led to a lengthy argument during which she had stooped so low as to mock him for no longer being able to afford to keep a helicopter. He had tried to explain that he had got rid of the helicopter because the fucking awful weather in the UK meant the thing spent its entire life on the ground denuding one of his offshore bank accounts, but this had fallen on deaf ears and she had simply repeated the fact that, whereas most of their friends seemed to have actually benefited from the recent recession, he was clearly on the ropes.

Now, after a tortuous drive during which he had engaged in an ugly spat with his chauffeur, they were arriving at the Holland Park house a good thirty five minutes behind schedule and he barely had time to work through a strategy in response to the company results which were waiting on the fax machine in his study. Dryesdale Ltd, the company his great-grandfather had built up from a small debt recovery business in the North East, had experienced a sudden and significant profit leap due to a rise in personal debt amongst low-income families. He was a little surprised at how long it had taken for this about-turn in his company fortunes to occur – debt being something that tends to grow in a recession - but initially he was more taken up with the thought that, with hard evidence before him that the recession was now working in his favour, he had for once won an argument with his wife. He handed her the fax as he passed through the kitchen, pretending to be on his way to the toilet off the downstairs hall, but he felt a wave of irritation as he heard her let out a whoop of glee on realising that they were likely to be several hundred thousand better off once the stock exchange had absorbed this news and acted on it. The significant point, that she was wrong and he was right, had somehow got lost.

Returning to the study, Mr Dryesdale's brow became furrowed as he began to get to grips with other consequences of this upturn in his company's fortunes. While the steep incline in profits would kick up Dryesdale's share value, the sheer extravagance of the profit rise meant that the left-wing press might want to spin together a sort of Marxist 'money from misery' story. Of course the fact that rather irresponsible and frankly stupid people had been buying monstrous televisions and three-piece suites in offensive colours when their incomes didn't warrant it would not be mentioned. Dryesdale's profits were coming from the 89% of these people who actually took the trouble to honour their legal repayment obligations. The 11% who preferred Drysedale (or at least their insurers) to take the hit for their irresponsibility would not be deemed of interest to the trendy layabout readers of The Guardian.

This was all more than just another irritant to Charles Dryesdale. He knew that modern governments were nervy, cowardly creatures that craved popularity at every instant. Critical press stories were like ghouls, skeletons and sudden unearthly shrieks on a ghost train ride. They were not there to be ignored but were in fact the entire purpose of the ride - there to be overreacted to. No sooner would stories appear than the government would be drawing up legislation to hobble his company with new regulations. Some years back there had been talk of making it illegal to hire ex-prisoners to make the door-to-door collections interest payments. It had given him quite a scare at the time and he had almost considered taking on one of the big PR firms to come up with some good counter-arguments. Ex-prisoners made excellent debt collectors because they tended to be quite thuggish, suitably tattooed and possessed of a certain *je ne sais quoi* about the eyes. To be barred from employing them would strike at the very heart of the Drysedale business model. Luckily on that occasion a terrorist atrocity of some sort had stepped in and yanked everyone's attention off in another direction and the threat of legislation had receded.

Now he was wondering if he hadn't made a serious mistake. He had Michael Peel and Associates to handle PR of course and Michael was certainly a safe old-school pair of hands. He had contacts in the City and could be trusted to undertake a low-key release of figures. More importantly he was likeable and had one of those trustworthy countenances that you could send ahead to soften people up. Cynthia liked him and Michael and Caroline had been to stay on several occasions, injecting some much needed social ease into some quite sticky mixes. But Michael was not a Machiavellian figure who could spin shit into gold. Those types tended to present you with the kind of bills that drained the colour from a man's face.

Now, he reflected as he dialled Michael's office number, he had no choice but to rely on Michael to handle this troubling situation and he had every intention of making him work for his rather modest fees. There simply was not time to properly brief a more substantial and cunning outfit.

Nigel recognised the world-weary and perpetually disappointed tones of the multimillionaire Charles Drysedale as he pressed the receiver to his ear. Mr Peel, who was seated opposite Nigel, could also tell at once that it was his chief client on the other end of the line because Nigel's figure became hunched and alert as he threw all his energy into trying to sound languid and at ease with the super rich.

"How are you Charles?" asked Nigel, "all set for the big day?"

His misjudged attempts at small talk irritated Charles Drysedale deeply – but they also irritated the hell out of Mr Peel, who held out his hand and shook it in a clear pantomime that demanded he pass the receiver immediately. The gesture both frightened and offended Nigel. In truth Mr Peel had forgotten, in the intensity of the moment, that he was currently a five foot eleven inch tall man of colour who was shaking a near fist at a five foot seven inch white racist with a chip on his shoulder. All he wanted to do was get the receiver so he could get on with dealing with the greatest challenge of the day.

"Good morning Charles," said Mr Peel when Nigel had passed him the receiver with a studied nonchalance. "Everything alright your end?"

"Michael have you even looked at these figures yet?"

Mr Peel felt his stomach turn to water as he realised that he had not. The last thing he had counted on was an actual crisis at Dryesdale Ltd. requiring some kind of expert PR response.

"I'm just looking at them now," he parried, as he attempted, with what appeared to Nigel to be actual violence, to search for the original fax on Nigel's desk.

"Just looking at them now? Michael its nearly twelve o'clock…"

Mr Peel did not hear the rest as he covered the receiver.

"For fuck's sake Nigel, where are the figures?"

Nigel fell into a form of paralysis at this. It seemed to him that this Mr Espadrille was now actually impersonating Michael Peel on the telephone, which was almost certainly some sort of criminal offence. What is more, a great black fist had been shaken at him and now the African had sworn. He simply didn't know how to process his sense of outrage. He managed to express a sort of baffled confusion, at which point the immediate crisis was averted when Mr Peel spotted the fax peeping out from under Nigel's copy of The Daily Mail.

Mr Peel whipped out the sheet and, with an eye practiced at looking at such things, he quickly identified the bottom line and noted that Dryesdale Ltd. had hit a boom time.

"I've got the figures here Charles," he announced with a burst of energy designed to silence the lengthy tirade coming the other way down the telephone line. "I see what's happened – the recession effect has kicked in. Congratulations."

"Congratulations?" Charles Drysedale howled. "The press are going to crucify us for excessive profits. What the fuck are we going to do?"

"We're going to thrash a few ideas out this end," said Mr Peel, glancing at his two colleagues for support and finding only that they were eyeing him as though he were a psychotic intruder and they his victims, tied to their chairs.

"You see this won't do at all," Charles started to say in an even more weary tone than usual. He was sinking into one of his deep glooms, where everything in the universe turned a sickly yellow colour, and all because no one understood him. "This is what I get for trying to support small businesses," he continued. "You've disappointed me dreadfully Michael – dreadfully. You should have your response prepared already – a range of responses. They should be printed up, with bullet points and highlights. It should be colour coded." He added suddenly, as though stumbling on the cure for cancer, "I simply can't imagine how you could have thought it was appropriate to be so idle on such a day."

The word "idle" constituted extreme criticism, even for someone as hard to please as Charles Drysedale. It had an awful ring of finality about it.

"There's something I haven't told you," said Mr Peel, preparing to produce what had proved to be his strongest card throughout the morning. "Caroline's had a turn - she's in the hospital. It's a measure of how seriously I take this that I have abandoned her bedside and am putting all our resources into dealing with this now. I really can't emphasise enough that we are preparing a measured response which will literally blast water at any press fires that might break out."

At the other end of the line Charles Dryesdale recognized that, for the time being at least, his sabre blow had been parried. The wave of irritation he felt at being asked to be decent when he was facing ruin washed over him with colossal force, and it was all he could do to stifle a groan. His irritation was augmented by Michael's fraudulent pretence that his company was some sort of collective of brilliant PR maestros who would now sit in a huddle brainstorming, when he knew perfectly well that Michael Peel and Associates was a one-man band. The thought of the idiot who had initially answered the phone having any input made him want to take a running jump into the Thames.

"I'm sorry to hear about Caroline," he managed to say, his voice cracking slightly at the strain of trying to sound sincere. He thought of adding the words: "I do hope she's alright," but couldn't quite muster the empathy. " I really do feel that we need to have a strategic response to anticipate…"

"I will have a strategic response," asserted Mr Peel, " but I think we should do it in a press conference – after the board meeting." The audacity of this suggestion made Nigel and Sackville cease pretending to work as they looked across at him. Charles Dryesdale, meanwhile, was momentarily reassured by the note of combative determination in Mr Peel's voice. Sensing that silence would terrify the man into superhuman effort, he hung up the phone without uttering another sound.

In order to appear dignified and in control, Mr Peel pretended that Charles Dryesdale was still on the other end of the line and said "Goodbye Charles" with a slight verbal swagger, as though replying to a friendly farewell. But when he looked across at Sackville he was met with the cold stare of a man of taste whose taste has been offended.

"I don't think that was quite the thing," said Sackville, whose heart was beating at twice its normal rate as he launched himself into the unfamiliar territory of open confrontation. Nigel, meanwhile, stared hard at his computer screen, secretly impressed at Sackville's previously unsuspected courage.

"What do you mean?" asked Mr Peel, with genuine interest.

"Impersonating Michael – it's not the sort of thing that's done – and I'm afraid I shall be duty bound to inform Michael of it."

Mr Peel straightened up some papers on the desk in front of him as he wondered how to deal with this very valid criticism. Sackville was certainly right that impersonating anyone in a business context was a serious 'no no'. The fact that he actually was Mr Peel and that he had not committed a breach of any gentlemanly code was of comfort only to himself.

"Briar you are right of course," he said, only making the situation worse by using Sackville's Christian name. "But I've always had the ability to impersonate Michael – it started at school – and he gave me his express permission to do it today, just to get things in hand."

"I'm astonished he never mentioned you to me," said Sackville.

"That's just like Michael," countered Mr Peel.

"I should say it wasn't like Michael at all," replied Sackville, who felt himself becoming quite upset. "Michael has talked at great length about his school days and has supplied character sketches of most of his contemporaries. I think I'd remember if he had mentioned a Henry Espadrille."

"Look chaps," said Mr Peel, changing the subject out of pure necessity and looking across to Nigel to make sure he was listening. "This is a mad sort of situation and I'm just trying to do my best for Michael. The point is that Dryesdale's shares are going to shoot up later and there's likely to be a media backlash because of the nature of their business. In my opinion, Charles is going to fire me… – I mean, of course - Michael - if I don't put my back into trying to make this operation run smoothly today. And any help will be much appreciated."

The threat of Michael being fired resonated deeply with both Sackville and Nigel, who well knew that Michael would not be able to afford the office rent without Dryesdale's business – forcing him out and them to accept a stranger into their midst.

"Why don't we call Michael and ask him what he thinks is the best strategy?" asked Sackville, picking up the telephone. Mr Peel froze in terror. At all costs he had to prevent any communication between Sackville and Caroline.

"That would be an excellent suggestion – but Michael begged me not to call. They have to keep the telephone line open you see, in case there are any developments at the hospital." Sackville looked momentarily doubtful – the faintest hint of suspicion beginning to haunt his face. "You can call him of course – if you want to," continued Michael, who, if nothing else, understood his colleagues' psychology better than his own mother, "but I'd hate to be the one on the line when the hospital called." He stood and moved over to Nigel's desk, taking great care to appear nonchalant as he delivered his closing argument. "Apparently if they get the engaged tone they don't call again for hours." Sackville cradled the phone unhappily in his hand for a moment, imagining being yelled at later for hogging the Peel family phone in time of crisis. He quietly returned the handset to its perch, coughing to muffle the sound of his defeat, then pretended to be suddenly busy with important paperwork.

For the next forty minutes Nigel and Mr Peel worked together on sending out the press release to the financial editors, to which they added the information that there would be a press conference immediately after the board meeting. Mr Peel also booked another room at the hotel – one that was suitable for the press conference. Nigel worked in a sulky silence while Mr Peel occasionally attempted to buoy him up with comments like: "You are brilliant, I never could get to grips with computers" and "How very clever you are" – remarks that made Nigel want to set about the dark- skinned impostor with an iron bar.

When Mr Peel departed Nigel and Sackville practically fell into each other's arms. They talked breathlessly about the various crimes against propriety and decency committed by Henry Espadrille before concluding that you could "never really trust them."

Meanwhile, Mr Peel walked the short distance from the office to the hotel in the City of London with a sense of rising panic in his breast. He was literally walking towards the lion's den without the least idea of how he was going to defend himself. The press would smell blood here and it was, by proxy, his blood that they would be smelling.

****

Mr Peel arrived at the hotel at 12.55 p.m. and found Charles Drysedale lurking in the foyer. Board meetings always made Drysedale nervous because the unceasing conspiracy to oust him as CEO of Dryesdale Ltd. generally reared its vile head at such gatherings and he felt that one of his many Achilles heels (his refusal to spend proper money on PR) was horribly exposed on this occasion. He knew the other directors were probably already hissing away to each other in the private boardroom hired for the occasion but he was keenly aware that without Michael Peel – who would normally have arrived early but was unforgivably late – he felt naked and friendless in a hostile world.

When he saw a mature and distinguished black man approaching him across the foyer with a film of sweat glistening on his forehead, he panicked and span around looking for fellow directors that he could employ to absorb what he felt was likely to be some sort of unpleasantness. He was uneasy around ethnic minorities. He considered them to be a largely untrustworthy lot and he had a deep conviction, drummed into him by a much-adored nanny in the 1930s, that black people in particular were lazy. Recently he had been put under considerable pressure to approve a policy of positive discrimination at Dryesdale to attend to the lack of racial and religious diversity at the company, which apparently was bordering on the criminal. This had all been presented to him on a day when he was suffering from a migraine and he had swatted it away as he might a large bluebottle, but he had been left with the uneasy feeling that he had set down an elephant trap for himself.

"Mr Dryesdale," said Mr Peel, panting slightly and struggling to disguise the immense anxiety he felt about this encounter. "My name is Henry Espadrille – I'm deputising for Michael Peel today because…"

"Deputising?" interrupted a wide-eyed Charles Drysedale. "Where's Michael?" he demanded.

"I'm afraid he couldn't come – his wife has had a turn."

"Yes yes I know about that but he never said anything to me about a deputy," said Charles Dryesdale, giving rein to mounting panic. "I need Michael here, now."

"I'm afraid her turn has turned…" began Mr Peel, "I mean it's turned ugly – Michael has had to literally rush to her bed side."

Charles Drysdale had gone silent and seemed to be looking at Mr Peel afresh. He was having one of those epiphanies that had marked him out, at least in his own mind, as a great genius in the field of business for more than four decades. His silence however, merely terrified Mr Peel, who was beginning to babble. "He's asked me to step into his shoes and take the handles - the reins - to grab the bull by the horns as it were…"

"So you'll come into the boardroom with me," interrupted Charles Dryesdale. "You'll be with *me* - and then you'll speak for *me* at the press conference?" As he spoke he willed the black man to say yes to these all-important questions.

"Certainly I'll speak to them," replied Mr Peel, falling quickly into the slipstream of Charles Dryesdale's enthusiasm. He had the giddy sense that suddenly everything was going extremely well.

"Well we must go in," said Charles Dryesdale, actually placing his hand in the small of Mr Peel's back in a gesture that, for him, suggested a huge upsurge of brotherly love.

"Where are you from originally?" asked Charles Dryesdale, by way of conversation, as they strode in tandem down a long corridor. The truth was it had occurred to him that he now had a man from a diverse background *actually representing him.* It was as if he had suddenly been given a magic shield.

"East Africa," Mr Peel found himself replying. The thought that a black man might originate in England was too modern an idea to occur easily to a man of Mr Peel's vintage. His heart did a somersault as he realised his African geography was extremely poor and he wasn't entirely sure which countries were in East Africa. Quite simply it was a continent that had never piqued his interest. "But I was educated at St. Paul's - with Michael," he quickly added.

"Perfect – so you're from Africa but you have an education." Incredibly a slight skip, not witnessed since university days, had entered Charles Dryesdale's step. "Now – I take it Michael has briefed you."

"Michael has fully briefed me," said Mr Peel as they stopped at the door of the boardroom. Charles Dryesdale turned to face his magnificent new spokesman and decided something had to be done about the sweat on the man's face. To him it suggested primitive terror.

"I'm sorry, what's your name again?" he asked, as he considered using his own handkerchief.

"Espadrille – Henry Espadrille."

"And it's *East* Africa".

"Yes."

"You've – you're…" He made hand gestures that spoke of water pouring down a face like rain on a windscreen. Mr Peel quickly pulled out his own handkerchief and dried his skin before refolding the dark blue cotton into a neat square and reinserting it in his breast pocket.

In the boardroom Charles Drysedale's array of fellow directors had indeed been planning a coup. They ranged from his smooth faced cousin who was aged just thirty-two and had a shock of golden hair to an elderly man who required an oxygen tank on wheels and was accompanied by a male nurse from Bangladesh. Despite the variety the board were united in their powerful distaste for the personal character of Charles Drysedale, who they all regarded as an appalling shit. The problem in the past had been that personally despising a person did not, in the highly pragmatic world of twentieth century capitalism, constitute solid grounds for turning on your CEO and forcing him to commit hara-kiri. But their current dilemma presented them with an opportunity to be rid of him that one of them had just been describing as "so rare and perfect that it was highly unlikely to reoccur in our lifetimes."

In short the likely press furore over their sharp hike in profits could be thrown off balance by the announcement that Charles Dryesdale's stubborn refusal to embrace new business practice had led him to lose the confidence of the board. Recognising that he could not continue to lead without the support of his peers, it would be solemnly declared that he had chosen to do the decent thing, in the wider interests of the company, and was delivering his own head on a platter. The column inches in the press would be dominated by the hideous tale of a great beast felled by the jabbing spears of his erstwhile colleagues, leaving little space to ask why a modern company was allowed to deploy convicted thugs on hard up families, concentrated in the depressed North East of England during a recession.

The particular sample of Charles Dryesdale's dangerously anachronistic management style that they had settled on to unseat him was his refusal to embrace the notion that the ethnic diversity of Dryesdale's employees should reflect that of the wider country. In short he was a racist and he should go.

It would be an exaggeration to say that the entire edifice of their conspiracy collapsed the very moment Charles Dryesdale entered accompanied by an immaculately dressed black man. What happened was that each of the board members recalibrated his position through a series of swift mental adjustments that began with 'Oh fuck,' and concluded with: 'Bugger - he's outmanoeuvred us.'

In fact by the time Charles Dryesdale had finished introducing what he described as "my new PR whiz and spokesperson," every man on the board had either decided that he would try to be the first to say something flattering to the CEO or would attempt to massage his ego indirectly by being particularly nice to this "Mr Espadrille." When Charles Dryesdale mentioned, with undisguised pride, that Mr Espadrille hailed originally from East Africa, his golden-haired cousin, a keen big game hunter who had a black rhino horn half ironically screwed to the footboard of his bed, leapt in first with what he intended to be a warm and friendly question.

"Oh I do love East Africa," he enthused. "Which country are you from?"

Mr Peel was not used to all this pressure. Ordinarily his day consisted of amusing banter with Sackville, telephone calls to old colleagues, pleasant lunches and occasional flurries of activity where his greatest challenge might be employing tact to get someone who was droning on to stop speaking to a room of near comatose shareholders. Now he was essentially disguised as an African, standing before the entire board of directors of a publicly listed company with the CEO beside him placing all of his hopes on his shoulders. And now his failing mind had gone blank about East Africa. If only he could go into a quiet corner and reflect on Africa in peace - then surely he would come up with a correct answer. But there was no time to think. He heard himself utter the word "Benin", and he instantly sensed that he had made an appalling mistake. The truth was that his knowledge of African nations, though crossword-friendly, was not intimately related to the actual geography of the place.

Practically every face around the table looked nonplussed. The cousin's head jerked as though he had been slapped in the face. Unable to censor his impulse to correct he blurted out:

"But my dear man that is in West Africa."

During the silence that followed Charles Dryesdale's head rotated sharply to the left as he looked afresh at the man in whom he had placed so much trust and hope. Was this Henry Espadrille just another blithering idiot, like so many of the others who had let him down in the past? He felt his buoyant mood collapse as a great landslide in his fortunes commenced.

Mr Peel rallied. It really was not on that he should fail now, over this irrelevant issue of which country he was pretending to come from. Inspired by the desperateness of the situation he launched into an outrageous conceit.

"You are accustomed in this country to thinking of yourselves at the top of the world – understandable. The first mapmakers would hardly think otherwise." He began - and immediately, and to his great delight, he saw that he was drawing them in and that he had a real chance to dig himself out of the hole. "In the little village that I come from we are very proud of our map-making tradition. As a chief of my tribe I am particularly proud that we made the first maps in the whole of Africa – not as early as the English," he added, finding it necessary to pepper a little flattery into the mix, "but they were good maps. Of course like yourselves we placed ourselves…" to illustrate he pointed into the air, causing several members of the board to look up to the ceiling, "at the top of the world – putting Benin, much to your current confusion – in East Africa. At least – that is how we saw the world."

Most of the board sighed obediently at being given such a fascinating and enlightening little lecture. One or two of them laughed pleasantly, in recognition of the charming way in which their Eurocentrism had been flagged up, but Charles Dryesdale sat rigidly in a cold sweat, reflecting that too much attention was being paid to this Espadrille character, a man he knew nothing about and who may have any amount of unpleasant surprises up his sleeve. He decided to wrest back control of the board meeting.

He began by announcing that Drysedale Ltd. had too few people "like Henry" and warming to his theme he stood up and began to pace around the table in a manner that his colleagues found menacing. "And like Henry," he continued, speaking directly at the young cousin who now seemed to be wilting slightly, the sheen even appearing to have dulled on his golden locks, "I want to turn our world upside down. The truth is that some of you have been stubbornly resistant to the idea of bringing people from diverse backgrounds into our company. Why?" he demanded and for a horrible moment it seemed that he really expected someone to answer. The cousin even opened his mouth but found that his tongue had completely dried up. "What possible reason could there be for excluding any part of that wonderful rainbow of colours and cultures that now make up this nation?"

"I trust," he intoned with some solemnity, "that none of you will object if I propose that we endorse wholeheartedly the recent suggestion of our HR department and introduce racial quotas into our next recruitment drive? It really is a little bit of a bloody disgrace that this hasn't happened until now." This extinguished any flickering remains of rebellion amongst the board. In fact they dared not look each other in the eye, so utterly trumped did they feel. Charles Dryesdale felt a dizzy rush as the tide of power abruptly turned in his favour. He even tasted a distinctive metallic flavour in his mouth. It was a curious biochemical phenomenon, which he did not entirely understand, but which was triggered by the sprawling defeat of his partners. It was his favourite flavour in the world.

The rest of the meeting was, in essence, an opportunity for Charles Dryesdale to consolidate his power.

****

Back at Mr Peel's office, Sackville had fallen into a bad habit. Some time ago they had had a television installed in one corner of the office, affixed up near the ceiling. The idea had been that they could check stock prices on Teletext. It also picked up the terrestrial television channels and it was hard not to give in to the temptation to watch daytime television on those not infrequent occasions when there was not a huge amount of business to be conducted. This usually occurred in the afternoon when lunch was being digested. Today Nigel had stepped out to pick up a sandwich and Sackville's lunch appointment with an old friend wasn't until 1.30 p.m. He found it impossible to concentrate on a press release he was meant to be writing and, tormented by the painful rumblings of his stomach, decided that he could justify the distraction of watching the one o'clock news.

The fourth item on the news covered the disappearance of Michael Peel from his home in Kent. As the story unfolded, Nigel entered the office with his sandwich while humming loudly. Sackville roared at him to be quiet.

It seems that Michael Peel had vanished and a black man had entered not just his family home but his actual bedroom, terrifying his wife. The item cut to a police sergeant with a tendency to use five words where one would have sufficed. He said that the police were keen to interview a man "witnessed behaving suspiciously and actually trespassing at the location where the incident occurred" and it was believed he might have information "pertaining to the alleged disappearance of the missing individual." He invited the public to call in if they saw the man in question, as the police were "anxious to interview him regarding his movements during the hours leading up to the alleged incident." The man in question was then illustrated with a photo fit picture, which obviously came from the fevered imagination of a middle- aged white woman who had been scared out of her wits. Although a great deal fiercer and more frightening than the black man that had rubbed shoulders with Nigel and

Sackville that morning, they realised at once that they were looking at "Henry Espadrille" as experienced inside the mind of Caroline Peel.

"What have we done?" asked Sackville, with great dramatic emphasis.

"Nothing!" squealed Nigel. "We haven't done anything at all. We can't be blamed."

"He's probably murdered Michael – buried him in the woods. Now he's at the Dryesdale board meeting – he's there now - just think what he might be doing."

"But what could he do?' asked Nigel with desperate, terrified curiosity. "I mean you don't think he's murdering the whole board?" The truth was that Sackville did not have the faintest idea what Henry Espadrille's wicked plan was – but there was an aspect of all this that was tormenting him. He could and almost certainly would be blamed for everything that happened in this frightful saga from the point where Mr Espadrille sailed out from the office. He had welcomed Henry Espadrille into the office, stood by while he impersonated Michael Peel on the telephone and set him on his way.

"We must call the police," said Nigel but his colleague's chubby hand shot up to deny the wisdom of this apparently obvious suggestion. The one thing Sackville was certain of was that he had to redeem himself. Nigel was a bit player in all this – a factotum of little more significance than a piece of office equipment. But he – Sackville – had been on the quarterdeck when the storm broke and had behaved like a blundering buffoon. Now he had to transform himself into the hero of the hour. Phone calls to the police were not enough. He needed to be on stage during the *dénouement*.

"We'll get a cab" he announced.

"Shouldn't I stay here and man the phones?" asked Nigel, who had started to believe that the terrifying photofit of Henry Espadrille was accurate. Sackville grabbed his arm. There was a limit even to his courage and it was essential he have someone to cushion blows should actual violence break out.

At the hotel a group of nearly twenty journalists had gathered in the room hastily booked by Mr Peel, where they were taking advantage of the free tea and coffee and quietly grumbling about the lack of pastries. The tables had been pushed to one side and more chairs than were needed had been organised into rows with a single table placed at one end.

When the board meeting ended the bulk of the board members joined the journalists as a show of support and solidarity. When Henry Espadrille approached the table accompanied by Charles Dryesdale, who was smiling broadly and seemed almost boyish in mood, the board members applauded warmly, forcing about half the reluctant hacks to join in (the rest being too hardened to be caught up in any form of enthusiasm). When the applause died down the press sat back expecting to be bored.

As he prepared to speak, Mr Peel was confident. The announcement of a recruitment drive and a programme of positive discrimination at Drysedale Ltd was an excellent way to demonstrate how increased profits were being pumped back into vulnerable communities through the creation of new jobs. To have announced this initiative as a white man, beside the white male chairman, with all the white male members of the board filling up the back row, might have seemed rather a feeble gesture deployed in desperation. To announce it as a black man felt highly appropriate and he doubted any of the hacks would be foolhardy enough to start giving them a hard time. He even felt a momentary panic at the thought that he might transform back into a white man literally as he spoke.

As he drew to the end of the announcement he relaxed enough to make a joke about how "everyone at Dryesdale Ltd is looking forward to seeing more faces like mine knocking about the place," a remark that produced a polite titter and caused the smile on Charles Dryesdale's face to alter, almost imperceptibly, into a grimace, as he realised that all this might actually have consequences for his company.

Mr Peel pulled his chair out and was about to sit when he glanced out of the window and saw, through a tall floor to ceiling window, that Sackville and Nigel were climbing out of a taxi. Sackville's expression was unmistakably that of a man on a mission to save his own skin. As they crossed the busy road Nigel glanced up at the window and Mr Peel dropped hastily into his chair, startling Charles Dryesdale and causing him to momentarily forget what he was doing.

"Shall we have a question?" said Mr Peel, his mind racing. He desperately wanted to make his excuses and leave. He was well aware that Sackville and Nigel were on their way to unmask him as the interloper who had murdered their colleague and terrified his wife. But if he walked away now he would ruin everything he had achieved through an incredibly difficult morning. Charles Dryesdale was actually happy, and in that rare state it might be possible, if not actually easy, to get him to write out a cheque. If he could just keep Sackville and Nigel away until he had got the cheque he could run straight to the nearest NatWest Bank and deposit it. His mortgage interest would be paid and Caroline would at least be able to carry on living in the house. He could then quietly turn himself in to the police.

The journalists were not particularly inclined to ask a question as they were sulking. They had been lured out of their various holes only to be fed a lot of very worthy fluff that, it had to be said, brilliantly neutralised any criticism that they might have cooked up. After a moment a woman in glasses asked if they knew what Dryesdale's "customer racial profile" was.

"We've got more than one customer," joked Charles Dryesdale – and actually got quite a strong laugh for his trouble. "But seriously," he continued, "we lend to anyone."

"At 4000%," chirped up someone at the back. It was a small man in a dark brown anorak who had gone largely unnoticed up to this moment.

"4000%!" replied Charles Dryesdale. "That's even better than my joke."

"It may be a joke to you," countered the man, "but it's not to the people that pay it – a loan of £1000 paid back over a five-year period comes to…"

"We don't want to get into this now," said Charles Dryesdale – looking briefly at Mr Peel and making a signal with his eyes, which translated as "shut the fucker up."

"You're running a loan shark operation that feeds on the desperation of the poor."

"Nonsense!" shouted Charles Dryesdale, slightly too loudly. He followed this with an attempt at a laugh but it came off badly.

"Pretending to laugh at the plight of the poor seems to me to be very bad taste," yelled the man. "Your profits are up forty five percent on last year because of unemployment – you are making money off misery!"

At this point Mr Peel heard the distant and muffled voice of Sackville yelling out questions far off in the hotel foyer. He turned to Charles Dryesdale and whispered, "I'm going to create a distraction".

"What sort of distraction?" he asked, with real terror.

"A man is going to come through that door talking nonsense – I will deal with him but…"

"What are you talking about? What sort of man?"

"A lunatic."

"I don't want any lunatics…"

" I'll deal with him but I must ask you to write Michael's cheque – for £12,000 – he needs it."

"I can't do that now," replied Charles Dryesdale, a line he would have used instinctively, even in the most conducive check-writing circumstances.

"Could we have an answer to my question please?" demanded the brown anorak.

Mr Peel stood up.

"Ladies and gentlemen," he announced, raising both his arms, palms facing the room, in a gesture demanding their full attention.

"Let's be honest - Dryesdale Ltd does lend money – and the rates are higher than the high street banks, higher than the building societies and even some of those debt consolidation companies that cold call you at home when you're in the middle of Sunday lunch."

Charles Dryesdale felt, for the second time that day, his world, like a great aircraft carrier fatally hit by Kamikaze pilots, listing horribly to port. He looked down at the table and attempted to throw his voice up and into Henry Espadrille's ear.

"What are you doing?" he hissed.

Mr Peel ignored him and ploughed on.

"But some people can't borrow from those companies – because they won't lend to them. And then where are they meant to go – to the local hood? Who charges ten thousand percent and rearranges your face if you don't pay? Dryesdale is a legitimate business providing a real service. It is profitable but the money doesn't all go one way. Right now – in front of you all – Charles Dryesdale is going to write a £12,000 cheque for a man called

Michael Peel – whose wife is sick in hospital and whose mortgage payment is hanging over his head like the sword of Damocles."

The silence that this remarkable speech gave birth to was soon filled with Sackville's approaching shouts as he argued with the manager of the hotel. In truth Sackville was deliberately giving ample warning to Henry Espadrille that his game was up so that he could run away harmlessly. The commotion, however, barely registered with the audience who were all watching Charles Dryesdale. Would he really write a cheque for £12,000?

Even to his own astonishment, the multi-millionaire found himself taking out a Coutts chequebook. Mr Peel whipped out a biro and handed it to him and after a last sickly grin, directed at the audience, Charles Dryesdale wrote out the cheque. As he signed it with a listless flourish the door burst open.

Sackville was red-faced and out of breath. Beside him stood the hotel manager, an insipid man who would take weeks to recover from all the excitement, and behind them both cowered Nigel.

"That man," announced Sackville, pointing at Mr Peel with a great sweep of his arm, "is an impostor and a murderer".

The word "murderer" had the opposite effect to that which Sackville had intended. It was simply too baroque and fantastical for the occasion, and it was met with a hearty laugh by the journalists. Charles Dryesdale and the board members recognised, instantly, that their press conference had descended into farce. The only person who leapt into action was a photographer (the only one present). He was a freelancer who had been advised by his agency that the Financial Times might want a picture of Charles Dryesdale looking either hunted or self-satisfied. He started firing off his Nikon.

Charles Dryesdale sat initially in an attitude of frozen horror but this evolved quickly into perplexion as he studied the red-faced Sackville, trying to remember where he had met him before (it was at the Beefsteak Club). Mr Peel stared at the chequebook, trying to calculate if he could grab it and rip out the cheque himself. A vision of removal men roughly handling his moth cabinet at Orchard House gave him the impetus he needed and he leant over his number one client, placed his hand flat on one end of the open chequebook and, with one swift jerk, he tore out the slip of precious paper.

For Charles Dryesdale having a signed cheque ripped from under his nose transgressed a fundamental universal law and he quickly looked up at the man whom he had, until very recently, regarded as his new public relations officer.

Before he could speak Mr Peel put his hand on Charles Dryesdale's shoulder, looked him closely in the eye and said: "This is a crossed cheque – the only person who can benefit from it is Michael Peel."

"Michael Peel is dead – murdered – buried in the woods in Kent!" yelled Sackville.

"It's all on the One O'clock News," chipped in an emboldened Nigel. Much to Sackville's annoyance this had a much greater effect than any of his own words. In fact Nigel's short interjection caused an urgent murmur to break out amongst the audience. The photographer doubled his rate of snapping, and focused his zoom on the face of Henry Espadrille.

Mr Peel's hand was still on Charles Dryesdale's shoulder.

"I can assure you that Michael is alive and well – but even if he wasn't Caroline needs this money to keep the roof over her head" he said. He was desperate to stop Charles Dryesdale from cancelling the cheque with a quick phone call to Coutts but he was actually barking up the wrong tree. Charles Dryesdale's mind was entirely taken up with animal terror. The hand on his shoulder felt like a steel vice and the tall black man now seemed to him to be nothing short of a psychopathic killer who had been stalking him for hours – and possibly days. He was not listening to a word that he was saying but decided to give him a sad and desperate smile, a complex facial expression that said: "you will have everything you require, and all the injustice you have suffered will be avenged, but you mustn't harm a single hair on my head because I am eye-wateringly rich."

It seemed to work. Mr Peel took his hand off the millionaire's shoulder, pocketed the cheque and began to stride towards the exit. This involved him walking directly towards Sackville, who tried to look brave while sidestepping to the edge of the room and colliding with a wall.

When Mr Peel reached the door he realised that he was, for the moment at least, a free man. But his innate sense of theatre urged him to make an exit speech. He not only had everyone's attention, but could almost feel that they were crying out for a rounded finish to what would inevitably become a favourite anecdote, retold into old age by all present.

He turned to face the room. All eyes were fixed upon him and even the photographer seemed to transform into a statue. The overall effect was like an incredibly dull exhibit at Madame Tussauds.

But what could he tell them? That he was not Henry Espadrille? That he was Michael Peel but with a new pigmentation? These, he knew from recent experience, were not facts that people digested easily. Then a thought occurred to him. He had a chance here to fling his pursuers off the scent – to deliver a red herring for them to waste their energies on.

"Tomorrow I will reveal the whereabouts of Michael Peel. At noon, in Trafalgar Square."

With that he departed – walking with long swift strides powered by an overpowering longing to get to the nearest NatWest Bank.

****

He was soon out on the street, where he quickly crossed the road and entered a small tobacconist's shop. The braver of the journalists, and the photographer, had followed him at a safe distance and they did not emerge from the hotel immediately. When they did, they scattered in all directions, craning their necks to see where he had gone. While Mr Peel pretended to peruse a display of carved wooden pipes he directed quick nervous glances out onto the street. He saw the photographer hail a taxi and depart, while the journalists re-formed and stood in a huddle. Whatever the content of their discussion the result was they headed, as a pack, towards Fleet Street.

"I use the Blakemar Straight Grain myself ." Mr Peel turned, startled, and saw that the tobacconist, a small bewhiskered man, had joined him at the glass display cabinet and was peering appreciatively at his own pipes. "I've never looked back," he added – but Mr Peel was already half way out the door, although, being well mannered, he did shout, "Beautiful pipes – must rush," over his shoulder as he departed. Once again on the street he quickly processed his mental map of the City of London. Remembering that there was a NatWest nearby he set off westwards.

As he walked he began to reflect on what Nigel had said in the last shambolic moments of the press conference: "It's all on the One O'clock News." What exactly had been on the One O'clock News? He noticed a woman in a matching pencil skirt and jacket, walking along the opposite pavement and staring at him with real alarm. She spoke urgently to a man who accompanied her and the man's eyes darted nervously at him. Mr Peel quickened his pace and felt an awful paranoia enveloping him. Was everyone looking at him? It seemed, in a terrible moment, that even those who weren't looking at him were thinking of looking at him.

He dodged into a narrow lane and then along a pedestrian alleyway. He would make his way to the NatWest through obscure side streets, passing as few people as possible. But when he emerged opposite the bank, after walking down another dark little alley, he was presented with a sight that caused him to fling himself back into the gloom.

Two City of London police officers were standing by their vehicle outside the bank, chatting easily to each other. Coincidence? Or were they waiting for him? He was overwhelmed by a desire to get away from the City. Word, perhaps, had already spread that he was here. He experienced a moment of real despair as he reflected that Charles Dryesdale may have already cancelled the cheque, that the police had already been informed that he was likely to try and enter a NatWest Bank. But this didn't quite compute. A man simply could not cash a crossed cheque unless it was written out to themselves – and what possible incentive did a murderer have to deposit a cheque in the bank account of his victim?

As he turned and walked back up the dark alleyway a grim thought occurred to him. Could they possibly imagine that Henry Espadrille had kidnapped Michael Peel, undertaken his PR duties for the day entirely to secure the £12,000 cheque with the intention of then getting Michael Peel, under duress, to withdraw the cash? It was too absurd. Surely it was easier to simply walk into a rural post office with a shotgun?

Emerging onto a main thoroughfare, he took a spontaneous decision to hop on a bus that was just then stopping across the street. He had noticed that it was heading to North London and would be passing near the home of his wife's aunt in Islington. Perhaps he could pay her a visit and collect his thoughts.

It was not a hopeless plan hatched unthinkingly in a moment of mental exhaustion. Far from it. In fact lessons learned many years before during his National Service were bearing long overdue fruit. Yomping about on Dartmoor in a persistent drizzle he had learned to think on his feet and utilise all existing resources.

Aunt Alice was of a breed of formidable English women; elegant without being feminine and underneath the pleasant exterior, as tough as reinforced concrete. Life had been relatively good to her until she reached her sixties, when she had suffered a series of misfortunes. Never blessed with children she had nevertheless enjoyed an enviable rural existence in an old parsonage in Kent where she regularly rode her spirited stallion, Bounce, and was an active member of the local Conservative Association. One day her husband John informed her that he had a secret vice, which was gambling. Races were his big thing; horses and dogs mainly but people and even boats suited him just as well. As long as things were moving competitively in the same direction he had an overwhelming compulsion to place a wager on the outcome.

Her first thought was that they at last had something in common. She too liked to watch the horse racing on Channel Four in the afternoon when he was playing golf. But his addiction was a morbid thing that gave him no pleasure, and her efforts to make light of the situation came to an abrupt halt when the full extent of the catastrophe became apparent. They were so in debt that everything had to be sold immediately. House, horse, furniture, jewellery, pictures – the lot. What is more, shortly after they had installed themselves in a one bedroom flat in a mid-period Georgian house on the unfashionable edge of Islington, John went up to bed for an after lunch nap and succumbed to a massive heart attack.

As if this wasn't enough, Alice had for some years been suffering from a cruel condition called macular degeneration. Never one to complain, the fact that she was increasingly seeing things only at the periphery of her vision was something that she took in her stride. Naturally she sought medical advice but, despite all the advances being made in other fields of medicine, it seemed she had stumbled on a disease that had left everyone scratching their heads.

Now in her late seventies she was completely blind and, being who she was, she was coping remarkably well. Eschewing a guide dog on the grounds that she was too old to learn dog-dependency, she got by on audio books, home delivered food, a few loyal friends, a procession of patient carers and good old fashioned British grit.

Mr Peel's idea of dropping in on her was extremely sound. Unable to see his transformed outer layer, Alice would simply be presented with her niece's husband Michael, a man with whom she had always got on very well. Coming, as she did, from a generation that was accustomed to making unplanned visits to each other (a last faint trace of a pre-telephone era), this would not raise her suspicions. Should she have listened to the news and heard of Michael Peel's disappearance then he would simply explain that the whole thing had been a misunderstanding.

In fact Alice had spent most of the morning listening to the talking books version of 'The English Patient,' and had enjoyed a pleasant lunch with an old school friend with whom she had polished off a bottle of Sauvignon Blanc. She could quite easily have drunk another half bottle without feeling in the slightest bit tipsy but the friend had left about 2.30 p.m. and Alice never drank alone. Instead she had settled in to listen to a bit of flat racing commentary.

On hearing a knock on the door she turned down the sound on the television and walked to the front door. "Is that you Roz?" she yelled.

"It's Mike," replied Mr Peel, who was nervously standing on the threshold, hoping that there were no twitching curtains across the street. "Mike Peel – I had a business lunch in the area and thought I'd pop in and say hello."

Alice opened the door immediately with a barrage of jovial insults about how he was rocking up, drunk as a lord, after one of his boozy lunches. In fact she was delighted at his visit and bustled him into the kitchen where she demanded that he have a drink with her. Mr Peel opened the wine.

Naturally Alice wanted to know how Caroline was, presenting Mr Peel with his first moral dilemma. Such a good old friend simply couldn't be lied to – and yet so much of the truth would only lead to unpleasantness. Alice was a good solid English type – the sort of woman that you could rely on to keep it together in an emergency, to endure any amount of hardship without complaining, and to do the right thing in pretty much any set of circumstances. But of all his friends and acquaintances she was, it had to be said, the most bigoted and unreasonable when it came to persons of non-white Caucasian race domiciled on British soil. Not that she was a member of the BNP or any other extreme right wing organisation, unless you counted the Farley Conservative Association. But the Farley Conservative gatherings were not a forum for discussion – merely an unthinking organ of support where she was forced to keep her views to herself. Her occasional rants about how the country was being taken over by work-shy blackies were heard only at small dinner parties given by her best friends, who long ago realised that it was best to just give her the rein for a few minutes and then guide the conversation into more agreeable territory.

Mr Peel hoped to avoid touching on the subject of his recent adventures altogether and would have preferred it if there had not been, somewhat absurdly for the domain of a blind person, a large mirror right there in the kitchen, a leftover from a previous resident keen to maximise the little light that seeped through the one small window. Seeing his black incarnation in this mirror he could not help reflecting on how very differently the scene would have been unfolding had she not been blind.

"Caroline's well," he replied after a moments hesitation.

"Oh dear," she replied detecting the uncertainty in his voice, "I don't like the sound of that – come on out with it - what's happened? You must tell me Mike, or I shall worry."

"No she's fine – really Alice – I only paused because we had a silly row this morning."

"What about, for God's sake?"

"Oh nothing important."

"Oh well, a row about nothing. We all have those darling. When I think of the rows I had with John. Of course they were about nothing too – nothing of any consequence. When I found out there was something to be really angry about it was too late to do anything about it so I was quite gentle with him really. Not that it helped, he popped his clogs anyway…"

Alice was a great talker and for once Mr Peel was relieved. He could simply let her chatter away, making occasional noises of assent while he pondered on what his next move should be. He considered calling his bank to see if a block had been placed on Charles Dryesdale's cheque but doubted such information would be given out, even to him. He had noticed recently that it was no longer possible to just call his bank and speak to his bank manager. He had even begun to suspect that his calls were not even being answered in his Tonbridge branch and the questions that he was asked to prove his identity had become increasingly complex and, it seemed to him, impertinent.

The only thing to do was to go to another NatWest and attempt to deposit the cheque. Photographs taken at the press conference might have reached the daytime news by now but he felt he had a good chance of completing the simple transaction without being recognised.

When he tuned back into what Alice was saying he immediately picked up on the word 'darkies'. She was having a bit of a go at them for keeping her awake at night with their 'radio cassettes' and taking much needed council houses away from the hard-pressed white working classes of Islington.

"Well why should that bother you?" he asked, in a gently satirical tone. "You're not planning to move onto the local estate are you?"

"I get the whole scandal from my cleaner Roz, I have to tell you Mike I get quite cross about it all – she'll be here soon - it is Friday isn't it? She's got three children all waiting for houses and she says she wishes she'd copped off with some blackie because then they'd have a damned sight better chance of getting fixed up."

The news that a cleaner was expected unsettled Mr Peel – especially as Alice was painting a distinctively unsympathetic portrait of her.

"'Scuse my French Mike but these bloody darkies pour into our little island with their hands held out, expecting to be in clover for the rest of their days without doing a days work – and we let them get away with it!"

Mr Peel, for the first time in his life, began to feel an unfamiliar sensation. In essence he was empathising with a whole segment of society that he had previously barely thought about for a moment. What is more it occurred to him that Aunt Alice was rather a malevolent creature. When she had lived in Sussex she had barely seen a black person from one year's end to the next, yet she had contrived to despise an entire race of people on the strength of a few Daily Mail articles and her own innate malice. The glaring image of the black man in the mirror in front of him, which he could not help seeing every time he glanced past Aunt Alice's right shoulder, seemed to demand that he produce some sort of balancing argument, but when he opened his mouth to speak he was interrupted by a sharp rap on the front door.

"That's Roz," said Alice, "You wouldn't be a darling and get the door would you? But for God's sake check who it is first or you'll have a blackie at your throat."

With a somewhat heavy heart Mr Peel got to his feet and entered the little hall. It was not going to be practical for him to hide from this Roz character and the only thing to do was deal with her head on.

"Is that Roz?" he called out.

There was a pause as Roz absorbed her surprise at hearing a male voice.

"Yes that's it," she eventually replied. He opened the door to find Roz extinguishing the stub of a Marlboro Light with the sole of her shoe. On seeing him she took a deep breath and nervously grasped her ponytail, instinctively tightening her hairgrip, which was already so tight it was effectively giving her a facelift.

"Is Mrs Hall in?" she asked.

"She's in the kitchen," replied Mr Peel," you must be Roz. I'm Michael – I'm married to Alice's niece."

This information threw Roz badly. Mrs Hall's niece could not be married to a black man, even one with a posh accent and a smart suit. If she had been then this would have been mentioned by Mrs Hall during one of their little chats – which so often touched on matters relating to race. But it quickly became absurd that she remained standing on the threshold and it was not really on to call him a liar. She was forced to square the circle with the thought: "with posh cunts any shit's possible."

Mr Peel indicated for her to step past him into the hallway and he shut the door.

"You there Mrs Hall?" called Roz, unable to stop her voice quivering with anxiety.

"Of course I'm here!" shouted Aunt Alice, whose hand was feeling its way across the table towards the half-drunk bottle of Cabernet Sauvignon. "Where the bloody hell else would I be – collecting cockles on Morecombe Bay?"

Roz let out a cackle of wheezy laughter on hearing what was one of Aunt Alice's favourite sayings, her relief at finding her employer at home and still breathing filling her with the joy of spring.

"I wanted to ask you something," said Mr Peel, choking Roz's laugher off at the source.

"Could you possibly tell me where the nearest NatWest Bank is?"

"There's one on the High Street, next' Tescos," she replied quickly and they both entered the kitchen.

"You've met Mike then?" said Aunt Alice as Roz made her way to a corner cupboard full of cleaning equipment.

"Yes," Roz replied – deciding that it was best to keep her answers short and get on with the cleaning rather than get drawn into a strange situation. But Aunt Alice was keen to demonstrate to Mr Peel that she had become very 'London' and was now on easy terms with the good old British working classes.

"I've just been telling Mike about the scandal of the darkies," she said, causing Roz to knock over a plastic mop bucket containing bottles of cleaning fluid and a washing-up brush. There was a terrific clattering sound, which made Aunt Alice jump.

"God that gave me a fright!" she exclaimed. Roz got on her hands and knees and began frantically gathering up the scattered things - and praying for a change of subject.

"I'm ever so sorry," she managed to say – her hand shaking so badly that she failed to properly grip a bottle of Mr Sheen and dropped it again. Her greatest terror was that she would make eye contact with the black man who was standing awkwardly over her. To avoid looking at him she kept her head unnaturally angled towards her breastbone as she reached for the recalcitrant cleaning product.

" I think poor Roz wants to get on with her work," said Mr Peel, noticing that Aunt Alice had spilled some wine. He grabbed a sponge from the sink and mopped it up. He was suddenly desperate to have a pee but he daren't leave these two women alone together.

"She can get on with her work in a minute but I want you to hear this from the horse's mouth," said Aunt Alice, "It's a bloody scandal and as a man of the world you ought to know about it – maybe you could write to the Telegraph or something – stir things up a bit."

"You don't want to listen to me when I get going," said Roz, "I talk a lot of nonsense. I don't know what I'm saying."

"That's rot," said Aunt Alice with real passion. "You shouldn't put yourself down Roz. You live at the sharp end of things and people need to know what's happening to the original and rightful inhabitants of these islands. The bloody Guardian journalists don't give a toss because they live in nice white middle-class neighbourhoods – but where Roz is she's under siege. What was it

you said? When you moved there it was a proper bit of London –
now there's so many monkeys it's like the jungle."

"Now – I don't think that's quite what I did say," asserted
Roz, finally forced to put up a rigorous defence. Everything was now
restored to the bucket and she bustled across the room, hoping to
knock the whole subject on the head before departing upstairs to
clean the bathroom.

"You're right you didn't say that - you said there were so
many *fucking* monkeys it was like the jungle – I was trying to spare
Mike's ears."

"Now I think you're taking me out of content," asserted Roz,
trying to sound serious and hurt. Mr Peel simply sat with his eyes
closed, waiting for the nightmarish situation to end.

"I never said that," said Roz with what she hoped was
unalterable finality and she departed upstairs.

"I don't know what's got into her," said Aunt Alice. "Usually
she'd be talking ten to the dozen by now." Her voice dropped to a
whisper. "On the whole she'd rather talk than work but I like a bit of
company to be frank – even if she is appallingly common. It's a
lonely business being blind."

Mr Peel felt that this uncharacteristic admission of
vulnerability presented the wrong moment to announce that he
needed the little boy's room – but he really couldn't wait any longer,
and he was keen to take advantage of the absence of Roz.

"I'll just be a second," he said. "Sadly I think I shall have to
get going after that but it's been wonderful to see you."

"And you Mike – and you," replied Aunt Alice, with real
warmth.

While Mr Peel was emptying his bladder Roz was smoking a
Marlboro Light out of the bathroom window to steady her nerves.
She was irritated because she had forgotten a large sponge which
lived under the sink in the kitchen and which she liked to use to give
the bath a once over. She did not particularly want to go back into
the kitchen and be forced to walk past a well dressed man that she
had effectively just called a "fucking monkey" but no black man was
going to stop her going about her honest work. With this thought
she angrily stubbed out her cigarette against the outside wall and
headed back downstairs.

On arrival in the kitchen she was surprised to find Alice sitting alone.

"He gone then?" she asked, squatting down and opening the cupboard under the sink.

"No no – in the loo," replied Aunt Alice, turning sightlessly to face Roz.

"Super chap Mike – awfully fond of him," she said.

"Seems very nice," said Roz, who had now retrieved the sponge and was ready to depart again. "You never mentioned he was a black chappie." She went on, in a sort of stage whisper, with one hand on the kitchen door.

"What do you mean a black chappie?" asked Aunt Alice, wondering if this was some sort of working class slang that she didn't know – perhaps meaning a person in a suit.

"You know a black chappie – a black man."

"Black man?" asked Aunt Alice with considerable gusto. "What are you on about woman?"

"Well he's black isn't he – you know – of the African whatnot - race – he's an effing darkie isn't he."

Even in the downstairs loo, Mr Peel got the full impact of the scream emitted by Aunt Alice, whose lungs hadn't been used for this purpose since she was twelve years old. It was a hideous dry screech, like a sudden forceful stroke across a rachitic old viola. Roz was sinisterly silent, although he soon heard the thump of footsteps and a clattering sound as a telephone was fumbled. Urgent muttering and the sound of a door being opened soon followed. He allowed himself the luxury of washing his hands and face, then emerged into the house. Aunt Alice was standing outside the kitchen, all her English courage mustered, waiting for him.

"I'm not afraid of you," she said

"I should think not," replied Mr Peel evenly.

"My God, what school of bloody infamy did you attend? To think that you would learn to impersonate a relative to get into an elderly blind woman's house! Well you've met your match with me young man."

"I'm sixty seven years old," he countered. "Look Aunt Alice, I am leaving now – I've stolen nothing, I've done no harm, and you know in your heart that I am Michael. It was very nice to see you and thanks for the wine."

"That voice," she replied, "it *is* Michael – it can't be anyone else – what has Roz done to me – has she lost her mind?"

"Don't be fucking stupid," interjected the harsh voice of Roz, who was half crouched on the other side of the kitchen door, "he's as black as fucking night." Emboldened by her own voice she flung the door back and was revealed to be holding a large kitchen knife, "Go on – I've called the police - now clear off out of it."

She menacingly jabbed the knife in the air towards him. He turned and fled.

****

Outside on the street the air was thick with the sound of approaching sirens summoned by Roz's earlier call to the police. Mr Peel broke into a run as he imagined the awful pity of being arrested with Charles Dryesdale's cheque still in his pocket, unbanked. As he rounded a corner, a police car pulled up outside Aunt Alice's house with an abrupt squawk of tyres. Another police car was shooting along the street he had just entered and to avoid being seen, Mr Peel dropped to the ground behind a van. He half crouched there for a moment, catching his breath and reflecting that he probably hadn't run like that for years.

He realized he was being watched by an alarmed mother with a toddler in a pushchair. Another slightly older child was standing unsteadily beside her looking terrified. All the woman's tigress instincts had kicked in and she was protecting her children with her arms as she stared coldly at him. The fact that he was blatantly hiding from a speeding police car marked him out as a very real threat. Embarrassed, Mr Peel made a cursory attempt to pretend that he was tying his shoelace. It was an instinctive gesture designed to give her something reassuring to say to her children but it also gave him a momentary illusion of dignity. He got to his feet stiffly, offered her a warm smile, and then crossed the street so he would not have to alarm her any more.

The main thoroughfare, Upper Street, was paralysed with traffic. Another police car had got stuck in an ugly snarl-up and its siren blared uselessly while lumbering buses performed tiny manoeuvres so they could release it.

Even from out on the street he could see that the NatWest was busy – a great snaking tail of people clutching papers in their hands. On entering, the entire queue looked at him and a man near the front, in paint-spattered overalls and holding an Evening Standard, was unable to disguise the thrill of seeing someone he recognised from the front page. He whispered to the woman ahead of him and held up the paper to show her the picture. She turned and stared wide-eyed at Mr Peel, saying "Bloody hell!" in a loud voice, before swinging around and trying to pretend she didn't exist. Realising it was hopeless, Mr Peel was unable to censor a loud shout of "Buggering hell!" as he departed, giving the queue members a short but memorable quote for later.

He walked back along Upper Street before ducking into Angel Tube station, an animal instinct telling him to get underground. There he bought an Evening Standard and disappeared into the bowels of London.

He used the newspaper to hide his face as he descended the escalator and experienced a complex set of emotions brought on by seeing a black man's photograph and recognising it as himself. From a variety of close-ups of Henry Espadrille the editor had selected a picture that portrayed him as profoundly confident and pleased with himself. "IMPOSTER HIJACKS PRESS CONFERENCE," ran the headline, "Police seek well-dressed chancer over missing pensioner". Mr Peel felt a surge of rage at the appalling insult of having an entire lifetime summed up with the word "pensioner". What was wrong with "ex-soldier"? "Loving husband"? "Father"? Even "PR man" would have been preferable.

Passing a map of the London Underground he stopped to examine it, realising that he had not decided where to go. The NatWest banks that he was familiar with were too close to his usual stomping grounds on the edges of The City of London, where the police would be on high alert for him. Clearly he needed to head for the periphery of London. Branches of NatWest were fairly ubiquitous but to be sure of finding one he needed a proper high street – not just some random bit of London that might or might not have one. On the map his eyes followed the cerulean blue of the Victoria Line downwards to its conclusion where the word 'Brixton' leapt out at him. A few years before he would have considered it a place to avoid – even in the guise of a black man. But the process of gentrification was well in its stride and even Mr Peel's son, Bill, had rented there for one six month period. Consequently Mr Peel had actually been to Brixton, although only for an evening, and he had taken a taxi afterwards to London Bridge station. He could hardly say he knew his way around – but after weighing up all considerations he came to a snap decision. In Brixton, surely, he had a chance of remaining at liberty for long enough to find a bank and undertake one simple transaction, before the full force of the law descended on him.

It was a long journey and he began to worry about the time. When did banks close? Was it five or five thirty? He had always visited banks after lunch and had no idea how their late afternoons shaped up. The time was creeping rapidly towards five and he considered simply jumping off at another stop – anywhere likely to have a branch of NatWest. But there was a saying he had learned in the army and it took a strange grip on him now: "Order, counter-order, disorder." It was better to stick with an original plan, even if circumstances changed, than to issue a new one. The thought of getting off somewhere completely random and desperately searching for a bank just did not stack up.

As it was he was attracting little attention. The tube train was extremely full and people were more concerned with retreating into their own little worlds. By holding up the paper to his face he was able to hide.

And naturally he was absorbed by the newspaper's report of his morning's escapades. The article kicked off with the mystery of the disappearance of Michael Peel. The insinuation was that he had been murdered, although they were careful to quote a police spokesman who said that "the body" had not been found and therefore it was wrong to jump to conclusions. The press conference was described as "chaotic", which seemed unfair to Mr Peel, who felt it had been well organised up to the point where Sackville had interfered.

They had clearly got very little out of Charles Dryesdale, who had simply issued a statement that his 'thoughts were with Michael Peel's family at this distressing time'. Reading between the lines, Mr Peel got the impression that Charles Dryesdale was actually quite pleased with the way things had turned out. The fact that a lunatic had taken over his press conference had completely overshadowed the release of his controversial company results.

Henry Espadrille was portrayed as a slick but sinister con artist whose motives were not entirely understood. There was an inference, delivered with some subtlety, that he was mentally ill and wanted to infiltrate a rarefied and exclusive white world for a day – although it occurred to Mr Peel that there were surely more exciting kingdoms to penetrate than the dreary world of financial PR. You'd have to be a very sick individual indeed, he reflected, to commit murder so that you could be Charles Dryesdale's spokesperson for a couple of hours.

The bulk of the article, which continued on page three, seemed to give an undue prominence to Briar Sackville and Mr Peel suspected that the journalist had been lured into one of his preferred drinking holes on Fleet Street, probably Ye Olde Cheshire Cheese, and there plied with booze and encouraged to see things the Sackville way. The sentence 'Mr Espadrille was violently grabbing millionaire Charles Dryesdale's shoulders when Mr Sackville exposed him and caused him to run away' carried the whiff of Sackville's vanity. Perhaps Sackville thought that by drawing attention to the man's wealth he would shame him into handing over a reward to his 'rescuer'. The absurd thought caused Mr Peel to burst out laughing – causing several heads to turn in his direction. He raised the paper higher to conceal his now famous features.

The journey to Brixton had a calming effect on Mr Peel and he emerged onto the street with the sense that victory was near at hand. There were many people about and there was indeed a predominance of black faces. Mr Peel selected what he felt was a harmless looking woman in late middle age and asked her if she knew where the nearest NatWest bank was. Terribly bowlegged and dragging a wheeled shopping basket, she came to a halt and scrutinised him as though he was something that had just risen miraculously from the pavement. "What's that you saying my darling?" she asked in a strong Caribbean accent. To his alarm two passers by stopped to watch this innocent encounter as though it were street theatre.

"I'm looking for a NatWest bank," he reiterated. One of the two people who had stopped to watch, a young black man in low slung baggy trousers that exposed several square inches of underpants removed his Walkman earphones and started to laugh. He touched the woman on the shoulder.

"Careful love, this is the geezer from on the news," he said and laughed again – looking openly at Mr Peel.

"What's that you're saying to me darlin'?" asked the woman, who was completely confused now.

"I just need the nearest NatWest." insisted Mr Peel – directing the question at anyone who might care to listen.

The young man now laughed again and exchanged a complex high-five with the other person who had stopped, a slightly older and more muscular black man with tightly cropped hair. Other people were stopping.

Mr Peel gave up and, seeing the way was clear, he crossed the street, followed by the shouted question: "You kill that man Mr Henry?" asked in hoarse voice by a homeless white hippy with dreadlocks who had got up from his post by the station entrance. To his relief, Mr Peel saw the familiar sign of a NatWest in the distance and headed towards it, reaching for the cheque in his inside pocket and feeling a surge of adrenalin as he prayed he wasn't too late. Several more people recognised him on the street – some paused and frowned, trying to remember where they had seen his face, others looked about on the street to find a 'normal' person they could talk to about their exciting discovery. Mr Peel got the uneasy impression that some people were actually following him.

He reached the bank's door to find it wide open, but as he stepped towards the welcoming void, a white woman with a pinched mouth and dirty blonde hair worn in a sort of frizzy bob stepped into the doorway with great officiousness and began to shut the door.

"Please – just one moment," said Mr Peel, wreathing his face in his most charming of smiles. "I know I'm terribly late but I have to bank this cheque or I'm going to miss a mortgage payment."

"We're closed," she said, continuing to close the door without pause, "the tills are closed."

"I'll fill out the form here and do a postal deposit…"

He never got an answer as the door slammed abruptly in his face.

"Open this door at once!" he yelled, and bashed on the door three times with his fists to drive his message home. "I said open this door. I know the chief executive personally and I will be calling him tomorrow. Tomorrow at nine thirty sharp. I'll be telling him how you treat your customers. Do you hear me?" he yelled again – but instead of the result he hoped for, which was the chastened and terrified face of the bank employee reappearing, he heard instead the sound of variegated sniggering from behind his back.

He turned to find a small crowd of people standing in a semi-circle looking at him with a mixture of fascination, amusement, and awe. A can of Special Brew had appeared in the hand of the homeless hippy and he wore a leer of joy on his face. He was delighted to be involved in a national event - the running to ground of a notorious, flamboyant, and genuinely bizarre criminal. 'He of the baggy trousers' (as Mr Peel now christened him in his mind) was also there, keen apparently to take a leading role as he stood slightly forward of the others, though his body language suggested he was ready to fall back should weaponry become involved.

"What you done with that bloke – you kill him?" demanded the hippy.

"Has anyone called the police?" asked someone else, hidden behind others.

"He's no murdering type is you me man," announced 'He of the baggy trousers'. "Look at the threads on him – he don't want to get no blood on his self." The crowd enjoyed this comment and responded with energetic laughter. More people were arriving by the second and there was much craning of necks. Mr Peel looked desperately for an escape route but unless he wanted to barge bodily through the throng he was trapped – practically pinned to the door like one of the moths in his display cabinet.

****

In Kent, Mr Peel's wife had had a difficult sort of day all told. She had been surprised in her own bedroom by a large mentally ill black man, suffered the awful anxiety of not knowing what had happened to her husband and had the immense irritation of dealing with the kid-gloved, patronising local police force. Worse had been the unspeakably forceful and arrogant members of the press who had quite blatantly driven up the short drive and started questioning her in the most insensitive manner and photographing both her and the house. Fortunately the police had now posted two officers at the end of the drive whom she insisted on supplying with a steady stream of mugs of tea.

Her 'community liaison officer' insisted on calling herself Jill and had an innately irritating personality. She informed her at about two thirty of the remarkable series of events that had unfolded at the Drysedale press conference. After that Mrs Peel had tried to speak to Briar Sackville on the telephone but he had behaved oddly – treating her as though she herself were a mental patient and then declaring that he had "several press interviews to conduct".

Two hours later, Jill the liaison officer had called again with a few scant details about the debacle at Aunt Alice's flat in North London. This had upset and embarrassed Mrs Peel in equal measure. As if poor old Aunt Alice did not have troubles enough of her own. Worse still was the thought that if Henry Espadrille knew Aunt Alice's address then he must know all their other friend's addresses as well. She remembered running from the kitchen as he was rifling through their telephone book and she felt an awful sense of guilt that she had not done more to protect the people she knew and loved. Who would he pick on next?

The only reassurance she had was that when she had spoken to Aunt Alice she found her in a buoyant and combatant mood. Delighted to have had all her prejudices about black people confirmed and, like Sackville, busy conducting a round of interviews with the press, she sounded more like someone who had found a new purpose in life than someone who had suffered a shocking ordeal. She even confessed that the Daily Mail was going to pay her quite a decent sum of money for an 'in-depth' account. However she wanted to be assured that her niece did not object to this. Feeling that this was the least she could do after what her poor woman had been through she willingly acquiesced.

At three thirty in the afternoon a van had arrived with police dogs and handlers and they had started searching the surrounding woods, using a shirt that Michael had worn the day before as a scent marker. Robert the spaniel had never known such excitement and would not stop barking. At first Mrs Peel had tried to distract him with treats but the animal simply ate while producing a sort of strange muttering sound – as if to say "I'm not able to bark at the moment but I will resume barking shortly".

She had then tried to lock Robert in her bedroom but the barking had continued and when she went up to check she found the dog with his head and shoulders out the window. At this point Mrs Peel had quite a serious argument with her son Bill, who had taken a day off work and had come down from East Dulwich to help her deal with the crisis. Bill had told her to "Stop fussing and let the dog bark," and when she had pointed out that she couldn't even think with the noise he had insisted on dragging the dog out and locking it up in the shed. She had protested quite forcefully that this was cruel, at which point Bill unleashed a passionate character assassination of the animal – pointing out that it had revealed itself to be a totally useless creature, having failed to alert her that a huge black man was on the premises murdering his father. Mrs Peel had then insisted that she would not have anyone talking like that while there was still hope.

She had of course reflected in the past on what it would mean to her if Michael died before her – he was five years older and had pretty much ignored all health advice. He was not a cigarette smoker but he had weaknesses for fatty food, good cigars, red and white wine and whisky. He was not one for playing sport or taking exercise and she had to admit that she was glad of this. The thought of him in shorts was too ridiculous. But the prospect of life without him was bleak.

What she was struck by, now there was a possibility he was gone for good, was how unbearably poignant his possessions were.

His dumb valet, on which hung his second-best suit with his-second
best shoes at its feet, had become a simulacrum of him – a cruel
taunting thing that possessed none of his gentle humour, his cheerful
nature or his ability to turn every misfortune into a well-turned
anecdote. Even an antique porcelain King Charles spaniel that stood
by the fireplace upset her, despite the fact that it spoke of his one
great character flaw. It was criss-crossed with myriad lines where he
had smashed it with the fire poker, then very inexpertly repaired it
with the wrong sort of glue. His notorious temper, *the red mist* as the
family called it, had been triggered by a row about money that
reached its crescendo when Caroline had rebuked him for spending
too much money on the ornament for her birthday. She often
wondered in what infant incident lay the origins of this temper –
perhaps a tit or a treat withdrawn at an inopportune moment? In truth
it was an inherited trait that occasionally missed a generation. A
great uncle had punched a subaltern in the Indian army after a
dispute over a missing pair of moustache tongs. Further back a great
grandfather had tried to mount the stage at a music hall in Bristol,
dreadfully provoked by a comedian who had ridiculed his baldness.
And on it went, back into the obscure past, a litany of red mists
descending into the flawed nervous systems of countless descendants
of Michael Peel. But the sight of the amber-coloured glue seeping
from the porcelain dog's wounds reminded her of his contrition after
the crime and his touchingly inept efforts to repair the shattered
object.

Worse still was the moth display cabinet in the kitchen. The
cabinet always conjured, for Mrs Peel, the image of Michael as a
little boy rising at dawn at his prep school in Warwickshire to check
his moth trap. He had long ago stopped putting moths into the
'relaxing jars' (as the killing jars were known) and then pinning
them into the displays. Nowadays he caught them simply for the
pleasure of naming them. Neither Mrs Peel nor their son Bill shared
Michael's deep fascination with moths but father and son had
bonded over a shared love of their English common names, which
possessed a colourful and poetic humour suggesting an earlier, more
amusing age. Names like the Flounced Rustic, the Chamomile Shark
and the Hoary Footman could be pronounced for the sheer pleasure
of saying them. Bill's personal favourite was the Setaceous Hebrew
Character. Of course you could not have a father with such a highly

developed interest in moths and not gain some level of knowledge and enthusiasm. Bill could identify some of the more showy species - most of them Hawk Moths (the Elephant, the Hummingbird, the Death's Head) and knew a few interesting moth facts that he occasionally served up at dinner parties if the subject came up; how some moths didn't possess mouths, the ability of the males of some species to smell a female from many miles away – and of course that great demonstrator of evolution, the Peppered Moth, which, over a few hundred generations during the industrial revolution, turned increasingly dark in hue to blend with the soot.

These days, after identifying a moth, Michael would release it. But now, Caroline pondered with grim humour, perhaps Michael himself had been 'relaxed' by Henry Espadrille. She was overcome with a sense of deep sadness, which she attempted to assuage by seeking out a very precious object. On their honeymoon in Italy she had found on her pillow, on their first night in the hotel, a perfect desert rose. How he had known that she loved this flower was quite beyond her, but she had been speechless with joy and had simply thanked him with a passionate kiss. It had ever since, she felt, remained their little secret. Much as she longed to ask him about it, the fact that it was never mentioned seemed to add to the intimacy and romance of that magic moment. She had kept the dried flower ever since, pressed within the pages of a five-year diary she had kept at the time. She sought it out now in an antique glass fronted bookcase in the bedroom. It had been a few years since she had looked at it but the diary was still there, a slight build up of dust on its top edge. It fell open naturally at the page with the great pressed bloom, which was now browned and fragmented. For all that she founded it deeply affecting.

In truth the flower had nothing whatsoever to do with Mr Peel and he was entirely ignorant of its existence. It had been placed there by the manager of the hotel, something he did for all his honeymoon couples, but by chance Mrs Peel had spied her new husband entering a chic little flower shop that very day and because of this piece of purely circumstantial evidence she had never doubted that he was the author of the romantic gesture. In fact he had only entered the flower shop because he was lost and needed directions back to the hotel.

When Bill had arrived at lunchtime he had not even removed his coat when he saw a dull grey moth fluttering about on the kitchen window. Without thinking he caught it in his hands. Normally he would have put it in a jar until it could be shown to his father. As Bill held the moth fluttering between his palms he remembered that his father was not there and might never be there again. "Here, I'll get a jar," Mrs Peel said before Bill could speak, and she retrieved one from a cupboard. As she undid the lid and handed it to him she told Bill to "Make sure we show it to Dad as soon as he's back – he'll love that." Bill smiled bravely, inspired by her optimism.

The irritating WPC who insisted on calling herself Jill had informed Mrs Peel about Henry Espadrille's promise to appear in Trafalgar Square at noon the next day. Jill advised her not to travel to Trafalgar Square as it was highly unlikely that Mr Espadrille would honour his promise and if he did turn up his arrest would, in all probability, be an upsetting spectacle.

But Mrs Peel decided that she would go to Trafalgar Square. It might be a chance to look Henry Espadrille in the eye and perhaps give him a piece of her mind. If only he had not surprised her in her bedroom, when she was in a state of undress and with a thick coating of face cream, she might have shown a bit more old- fashioned British spunk.

When the light started to dim at around four thirty the police dogs were all loaded back into the van and Robert was finally released from the shed, his tail wagging so violently that he almost unbalanced himself and fell over in the kitchen. The failure of the police dogs to find a shallow grave in Bluebell Wood was excellent news but the search was to continue the next day. Bill had agreed to spend the night with his mother and he had a long phone conversation with his wife in East Dulwich while Mrs Peel prepared her traditional 'crisis' meal (kedgeree), occasionally taking sizeable sips from a gin and tonic.

****

Leslie Marsh had shut the door of the NatWest Bank, Brixton Road branch, as she did every working day at five o'clock to stop people entering after the tills had closed. She was used to irate customers getting bolshy at being denied entry at this time and could never understand why people could not take the trouble to find out what their opening hours were. Today an alarming black man had bashed on the door and shouted threats – and she had considered calling the police, before quickly realising that this would only delay her return home to Weybridge where Jeff, the beloved tomcat, waited in agonies of greed. Did these people think that bank employees worked twenty-four hours a day? Everyone was so rude these days.

In fact the door Mr Peel bashed on was the only way out of the bank and as, one by one, the various assistant managers, under-managers, clerks, IT people and other employees finished their work for the day, they gathered on the other side of it and waited for Leslie to release them. Normally she would stand letting them out in dribs and drabs but there was a bit of a commotion on the street outside and it was agreed by straw poll that they would wait for things to settle down. Somewhat defiantly an impatient young man with almond wax in his short mousy hair climbed on a chair and looked through a high window. "There's just loads of people around the door," he reported, and another employee, a buxom black woman in her thirties, climbed up beside him to take a look. There was not room for them both on the chair and the mousy haired man was shoved off.

"There's this black bloke in a suit and stuff – he's sort of like talkin'," she said. "Everyone's like hasslin' him and that."

Leslie assumed that it was the same man who had bashed on the door and she told them that she knew for a fact that he was violent, before adding: "Casey if you fall off that chair you'll sue me for not telling you to get down."

At this point the bank manager joined them, a shy serious man of Somalian parentage. Approaching the door he removed his clear-rimmed spectacles and cleaned them with a tissue while quietly demanding to know what was going on. When he had been apprised of the situation and had subtracted the tendency towards hysteria common amongst his staff, he ordered Leslie to unlock the door immediately so they could all go home.

Out on the street Mr Peel was waiting to be arrested. The crowd of people were not being aggressive but there were too many of them for him to be able to break through and he really had no idea where to go. Even if he could find his way to a hotel the staff would likely call the police as soon as they saw him and even if they did not there was a good chance his bank cards had been cancelled and he wouldn't be able to pay for a room. His chief concern, now that he had accepted defeat in his efforts to bank the cheque, was that he was hungry. He had eaten nothing since the sandwich on the train in the morning and although the excitements of the day had kept his mind off his gut until now, it had begun to demand its due. Once in police custody, he reflected, it might be hours before anyone thought to offer him a meal.

The homeless hippy and 'He of the baggy trousers' had become the unofficial showmen and guardians of the free public freak show that was Henry Espadrille. A constantly shifting swarm of people struggled to the front to see what the fuss was about, then stared in amazement at a real live national news story in the flesh. First the hippy, then 'He of the baggy trousers' took turns in giving snatches of commentary. Occasionally they would throw a question at Mr Peel.

"Come on – 'fess up - you kill that man or not?"

Mr Peel ignored them at first and then began to answer in a mild and reasonable tone to help pass the time. His answers delighted the crowd – chiefly because of his posh accent. "Are you going to hand yourself in to the police?" asked someone. "I seem to have handed myself over to the mob" (cue: burst of laughter). There was something unreal about the situation and his hunger had made him light headed. He was about to sit on one of a pair of shaped concrete blocks that jutted out on either side of the door, when he heard the sound of the lock behind him being unfastened.

The bank employees had not agreed on a tactic but when it came to it they all left at once – bursting out of the door like people leaving a burning building. The crowd stepped back and gaps opened up to allow them through. The bank employees did not even see Mr Peel, who was half-crouched near the door's hinges. In fact the door itself concealed him as it flew open. Taking advantage of his momentary invisibility he made the decision to join the departing workers. Before he knew it he was striding along Brixton Road and when he glanced back he saw that the crowd was looking baffled, as though he had vanished in a puff of smoke.

The bank manager was the sort of man who liked to keep himself to himself and although he was aware that a mature, well dressed black man was walking in step with him he avoided looking directly at him and then took evasive action – stepping to the edge of the high street and using a brief gap in the traffic to cross the street. Mr Peel, however, felt that the fine featured man, with his glasses and deep frown, provided an excellent natural mask and he crossed the road with him. Having arrived at the other pavement, the bank manager came to a halt and stood with his arms at his side, hoping that the man would walk away, but Mr Peel stopped too. The bank manager now looked at Mr Peel. "Can I help you with something?" he asked.

"Is the bank open on Saturday morning?" asked Mr Peel. "I need to deposit a cheque". The manager examined Mr Peels face for a moment and, seeing that the query seemed to be genuine, he told him that the bank was open from nine o'clock – then wished him a good evening and strode away, leaving Mr Peel alone and exposed. He heard the sound of police sirens approaching and looked about for somewhere to hide and, ideally, eat. Further along the street he saw a large Victorian pub.

****

The pub was almost empty, with one man playing a fruit machine and another drinking a pint of cider and muttering to himself. Neither turned to look when Mr Peel entered and there were no bar staff visible. Treading quietly, Mr Peel headed straight through the cavernous interior with its strong odour of ale soaked timber and into the men's toilets, where he went into a booth and sat down. Should he have just waited to be arrested? The thought of spending a whole night on the run in London was too horrible. But as well as his hunger there was the instinctive yearning for freedom and a horror at the thought of interrogation. A great deal of unpleasant police sarcasm was likely to rain down on his head once he started answering their questions. What is more, handing himself in was not going to assuage the suffering of poor Caroline – hearing that Henry Espadrille was still claiming to be her husband could only upset her more. He might as well remain at large as long as he could.

With its gentle hissing of pipes and dripping of cisterns, the toilet was a surprisingly peaceful place to collect his thoughts. It had been recently cleaned, so it smelt of disinfectant rather than anything more unpleasant. Next door he could hear that the pub was getting busier as people filtered in after work. It suddenly occurred to him that he was desperate for a crap.

He was enjoying a thoroughly successful bowel movement when he heard the pub go suddenly silent – followed by the muffled fizzle of a police radio. Voices were murmured, questions were asked. How thorough would they be? If no one saw him enter the pub would they really go as far as searching the toilets? Mr Peel's heart sank to its lowest ebb of the day. What a sordid fate – to be arrested on the loo.

But then the hubbub in the pub resumed, louder than before as people discussed the police visit. Mr Peel finished his business and exited the booth. He washed his hands and then waited by the door until he heard the fruit machine chugging out a few coins. As a distraction it would have to do.

There was a small booth near the door at the other end of the bar and he walked towards it while looking down and pretending to pull a piece of lint off the lower part of his suit jacket. The barman looked over at him but the animated chatting amongst the customers continued. He removed his jacket and put it on the back of a chair facing the wall and then approached the bar.

"I was wondering if I could get something to eat," he said. The barman was an Australian with a scar on the side of his head from where the pointed end of a surfboard had smacked into his skull on a windy Indonesian foreshore. He felt a dim sense that this black man was connected to something that had happened earlier, but failed to join up the dots. "We have a full bar menu, sir, but I can tell you for nothing that the sausages are reeeaaallly good."

Mr Peel completed his order – paying with cash, then sat down with a pint of bitter and a packet of peanuts. People came and went, the food arrived and he began to eat with a fierce appetite. He was half way through the meal when he found a man standing next to him with an expression of polite apology.

"Do you mind if I sit there?" he asked, indicating the chair opposite. He was a black man but with paler skin than Mr Peel, and short neat dreadlocks that fanned out from his head, giving him the look of permanent surprise. He was about thirty-five years old.

Mr Peel didn't answer and the man felt compelled to explain. "I always sit at this table, circumstances permitting," he said. Although this explained nothing, Mr Peel indicated with his hand that he was welcome to the seat. He would have spoken but his mouth was stuffed with Lincolnshire sausages and mash. "Thank you," said the man, moving towards the bar as he spoke. "What's that your drinking – Theakstons?"

When he returned with the drinks Mr Peel again had a mouth full of food.

"There's a man with a healthy appetite," said the man, settling into his seat.

"I was extremely hungry – I missed lunch today," replied Mr Peel after he had taken a generous swig of Theakstons.

"I'm Dave," said Dave, holding out his hand. There was an awkward moment as Mr Peel wondered which name he should use. He decided he was too tired to be anything other than himself.

"Michael," he said, shaking Dave's proffered paw.

"Good evening to you Michael," replied Dave, using a formal manner of speaking that was a quirk of his.

"I regard this seat as something of a good luck talisman so I appreciate you letting me perch here. I run the show upstairs, as it happens – and showbiz breeds superstition. Yes its all true – we're all as flakey as a pack of pork scratchings."

"What's the show upstairs?" asked Mr Peel.

"The show? The *show*," added Dave, placing serious emphasis on the word to suggest it was the most important thing on earth – but at the same time wearing an ironic expression on his face to convey the opposite meaning. "I take it you are not a regular in this fine hostelry?"

"No I'm afraid not – first time I've been in here."

"Aaah well, I can't say it's been your loss. The show upstairs is a sort of Friday night talent contest with a sprinkling of one or two – or three if we're lucky – semi-professional performers. Very popular on account of – punters are often related to the acts – or their friends if you follow. This has the benefit of putting bums on seats."

Mr Peel was starting to like Dave. His manner of speaking, combining a sort of old-world formality with straight–to-the-point bluntness appealed to him. Dave also possessed a natural warmth that made Mr Peel feel at home and he was enjoying, for the first time in his life, the feeling of being on easy terms with a person of another race. Of course there was also the added bonus that Dave didn't seem to recognize him from the newspaper.

A quite different set of thoughts were running riot in Dave's mind. At first he had been intrigued to find himself sitting with what was clearly a privately educated black man. He had met them before but never one this old, and never one who inhabited the role of the English gent with such conviction. Then he had realized, with a sudden shock, that he was having a drink with Henry Espadrille, the chancer and possible murderer from the news. This, of course, changed everything.

"So how did you come to miss lunch Michael?" asked Dave – feeling that this gave Henry the opportunity to open up if he felt that way inclined.

"I've had a very difficult sort of day   but I wont bore you with it."

"Bore away," parried Dave, "I always get here early because I never know what sort of state the upstairs room is going to be in. Take last week for example. There'd been a hen party the night before and I had to pick up God knows what – I'll spare you the details as you're still eating your dinner. Tonight however, the entire room is pristine and ready, meaning that I now have time to kill. Anything to take my mind off the show is a very welcome distraction – I still get nervous as it happens."

"Well if I'm doing you a favour then I'm happy to oblige but I will tell you this in advance – you are not going to believe a word I tell you."

"You seem very sure of that," Dave replied, very conscious that he was dealing with a confidence trickster whose every utterance was likely to be a ploy.

"I'm certain of it," countered Mr Peel, " in fact you are going to regard me as a deluded lunatic."

"This sounds right up my street – fire away sir."

Mr Peel smiled at this and for a moment they looked each other in the eye. Dave had one of those faces that suggested he was on good terms with the world. Mr Peel felt like unburdening himself of his terrible ordeal.

"This morning," began Mr Peel, "I awoke as usual in my house in Kent with my wife Caroline. Everything was as it always is – with one detail changed. In the night I had transformed into a black man."

"Might I enquire as to what colour you were you when you turned in?" asked Dave, with barely a pause.

"White," said Mr Peel.

"White!" repeated Dave – as though uttering the answer to a crossword puzzle that had been eluding him for an age. This was even better than he had hoped – infinitely better. The man was totally barking.

"So presumably your wife had a thing or two to say about this?"

"She immediately became completely hysterical," replied Mr Peel and Dave found it necessary to bite down on his tongue to stop himself laughing. He looked down at a beer mat and pretended to read the wording. Tears formed in his eyes.

"Are you alright?" asked Mr Peel.

"I'm fine," replied Dave and he managed to indicate that he needed to take a leak.

In the toilet he stood propping himself against the wall with one arm outstretched, trying to get a hold of himself. It was relatively easy not to get the giggles standing here alone in the bathroom but what would happen if he roared with laughter when he was once again seated opposite his new friend Henry Espadrille? Henry might take offence. He had already killed once – having someone laugh at him might provoke him to kill again. But this was priceless stuff.

When he again took his seat he saw that Mr Peel had bought him another pint.

"Thanks for that my friend," he said.

"Please don't feel that you have to go to the loo every time you need to laugh at me," said Mr Peel.

"It's a fair cop gov," replied Dave, with surprisingly little embarrassment. "Alright I'm going to level with you – I don't believe you. And I do know who you are. You're Henry Espadrille – whose faced is smeared across the Standard."

"Why on earth are people prepared to believe in a ridiculous name that I made up in a panic this morning?" asked Mr Peel.

"Well tell me your real name and I'll happily use it," said Dave.

"I told you my real name – it's Michael, Michael Peel."

"Alright look," said Dave, who felt, on balance, that whether this was Henry Espadrille or Michael Peel, the man seemed unlikely to start wielding an axe. "I admit I was having a bit of a giggle in the bogs but I would very much like to hear more about your day. I take a personal interest in your tale as a student of race relations and – I am prepared to add - an aficionado of comedy. If I laugh I'll laugh openly without retiring to the conveniences."

Mr Peel sighed – his tragedy had been reduced to a vaudeville act for the benefit of one man. Then a thought occurred to him.

"I don't mind you having a laugh at my predicament but in return perhaps you could do me a favour."

"What favour's that?"

"I'm completely stuck for a place to stay. Can you put me up for the night?"

Dave fell silent. He was not in the habit of accommodating nutters in his small Kennington flat.

"If you don't I will just turn myself in to the police. In fact I'll do it after I've finished this pint. I really don't have any particular reason not to," continued Mr Peel. "They are never going to find Michael Peel's body because I am not dead. I have not committed any crime. I have not stolen anything or hurt anyone. I might as well get it over with and turn myself in."

"So why haven't you?" asked Dave.

Mr Peel took the cheque from his pocket and handed it to him.

"That cheque, written out to myself, needs to be deposited at NatWest bank urgently, otherwise we are going to default on our mortgage payment and we'll lose the roof over our heads. I missed the bank today because I have been barely able to stay one step ahead of the law. I'm too old to cope with sleeping rough tonight. On balance a police cell is preferable."

Dave examined the cheque carefully. £12,000 was a lot of money. It was a crossed cheque – he knew what that meant – and it was indeed written out to Michael Peel. Coutts and Company was about as posh as it got.

"Isn't that the Queen's banker?" said Dave, who knew a thing or two.

Mr Peel nodded. "At the press conference I told them I'd be at Trafalgar Square tomorrow morning at noon. If you'll put me up I'll do just that – after I've been to the bank."

"You'll hand yourself in tomorrow in Trafalgar Square?"

An idea was forming in Dave's mind.

He had a day job as an electrician and he did not enjoy it. In the evenings he traipsed up and down the Greater London area, and occasionally made forays out to little venues in the wider country, performing in venues of every description, usually unpaid. He was a stand-up comic and his career had stalled. He'd seen younger and less talented comics come into the business and then swiftly overtake him. He was starting to get fed up.

What he lacked was exposure – and now he saw an opportunity.

"I've got a suggestion," he said, handing the cheque back to Mr Peel. "I suspect that you are profoundly ill but on the plus side you are so utterly convinced of your delusion that you are — for now at least – stable and of no immediate danger to the general public, and, more importantly, to myself - in my non-professional and completely ignorant opinion, which counts for a great deal with me."

"Thank you - I suppose that's a compliment of sorts," replied Mr Peel dryly.

"You're welcome," said Dave cheerfully. "What I'm thinking is – we have a bit of a Henry Espadrille themed evening upstairs. All I mean is – I'll do some material around the story. Most of the audience will be black so it's going to have a certain resonance with them. Then for the finale – we bring on – ta da," he flung his arms out towards Mr Peel in a theatrical flourish, "The real Henry Espadrille!"

"At which point I come on stage? And do what exactly? I don't know any jokes"

"Just talk about your day – starting as you did to me just now and going on in that vein. Keep it down to five, maybe ten minutes, – bam – blow their tiny minds."

Mr Peel felt keen disappointment. The idea of finding somewhere to stay the night had been attractive. He'd be able to bank the cheque in the morning – a great victory plucked from the jaws of defeat. But this Dave character was charging too high a price. He wanted him to endure public humiliation.

Dave could see that his idea was going down badly.

"It was just a thought," he said.

"Well as thoughts go I'd say it was a pretty grotesque one."

"Grotesque," replied Dave, savouring the word. "Nice vocab. I apologise if my suggestion offends you. The truth is I'm actually complimenting you. People fall over themselves for my ten minute comedy spots."

"I am not a comedian," said Mr Peel. "I'm a respected Public Relations executive who turned black in the night."

Again Dave had to bite down on his tongue – almost making it bleed.

"Knock yourself out," said Mr Peel, "I told you that you're free to laugh at me."

Dave got a hold of himself. He used a napkin to dry his eyes and decided on a new tack: begging.

"Michael – I'm desperate," he began. "I've been performing stand-up comedy for six, no – seven - years. Christ I've been doing the show upstairs here for two years. The thing is, I'm good. I promise you I am good – I'm very good. But I've never had a break. You need a break in this business. You could be my break."

"How so?"

"Because the press will be all over this like the Daily Mail on a bigamous Nigerian benefits scrounger."

"But how will that help you – the press will surely be writing about how the renegade Henry Espadrille had the audacity to start treading the boards – at best you'll be a detail."

"But this is show business!" cried Dave. "If Henry Espadrille is in a show then everyone will want to know which – if you'll excuse my Esperanto – fucking genius put him in the show. The answer is written on the backdrop behind your head – I mean on the stage," he added, stopping Mr Peel from turning to look behind him.

"But surely someone will call the police as soon as they see me on stage?"

"What this lot? Unlikely," Dave replied, but then he seemed to give serious thought to this danger. "Well they might," he admitted. "But I'll have them primed up and on your side by the time you appear. I can't really see anyone calling the old Bill while you're on stage because, believe me, they'll want to hear what you've got to say. And after that we'll be making ourselves scarce anyway."

"So if I agree to this you are inviting me to stay?"

"You're not gay are you?"

Mr Peel chose to ignore the question.

"So as far as you're concerned – I'm just a chance for a bit of free publicity?" asked Dave.

"Yes – in a nut shell. I've got a mate – Keith – who sometimes films the shows. He makes a few quid running VHS tapes off for the acts – he takes photos too. I'll give him a bell and get him to film the goings on tonight. I know for a fact he's sold stuff to the BBC so maybe he can get us on the news. Which means your face and, all going well, mine, beamed into the homes of the good people of these islands."

"There's no such thing as bad publicity," said Mr Peel.

"I'll come with you to Trafalgar Square as well – make sure there's no police brutality. Of course I'll be mugging for the cameras there as well."

"So this is what naked ambition looks like," said Mr Peel.

"Ugly isn't it?" replied Dave with a grin.

Mr Peel contemplated his plight. What on earth would he be letting himself in for if he said yes? It was quite possible that a crowd could turn ugly if he appeared to be revelling publicly in his notoriety. He was, after all, accused of murder. But there was another side to all this. Mr Peel was not a stranger to public speaking. Over the years he had made more speeches than he could possibly count and he was rather good at it. In fact he had something of a reputation for making short amusing speeches that still managed to stick to the dry and tedious subjects that he had been forced to speak on. On more than one occasion he had regretted that he had not made more of this ability and branched out into speaking on more entertaining subjects. Now he had an astonishing story to tell.

When their drinks were finished they went upstairs to the events room. It had a long wooden bar running almost the entire length of one side and a small stage at one end. Dave got to work setting up the microphones and doing sound tests and after a while performers started drifting in. There were three young black singers, one of whom disappeared into the upstairs toilets where she could be heard warming up her voice. A second generation Tamil Indian comedian helped Dave move a pair of heavy speakers and two other comedians, one black, one white, drifted in and sat at the very back of the room, languidly discussing their recent gigs until Dave introduced them to Mr Peel.

The three amateur singers were too nervous and preoccupied to notice the notorious Henry Espadrille, and the comedians, being unshockable, simply recognised his presence as a showbiz coup. In fact they began excitedly circling Mr Peel and explaining why they needed to have their photograph taken with him. Dave stepped in and after some negotiation it was agreed that when Keith arrived he would take one posed picture of each of them with the notorious con artist, for which they would pay him his standard rate of seven quid.

Dave felt that, while the house lights were up, Mr Peel should hide from the audience. There was a wide alcove in the wall opposite the bar, which acted as a cupboard for all sorts of junk and he suggested they put a chair in there. But while they were inspecting the alcove they found an old folding screen. They set it up at the back of the room, next to where the other performers would sit during the show.

The audience began to trickle in just before eight, paying four pounds fifty to Dave who was seated at a little table by the door. At this point Keith arrived lugging several bags of equipment. He was wizened and almost toothless (the result of heroin addiction) and he was in quite a state – pale as a peeled turnip and glistening with sweat. He contrived to show little interest in Mr Peel but in fact he was extremely excited. The Henry Espadrille story was huge and Dave had handed it to him on a plate. He had already called several media agencies and had sold, in advance, the photographs and video footage he was planning to capture for several thousand pounds. He had of course refused to divulge where Henry Espadrille was going to appear and had taken an extremely circuitous route to the venue – a route that had become positively Byzantine as his natural inclination to paranoia had taken hold. At one point he had travelled all the way to Mornington Crescent in a determined bid to shake off what he was convinced was a journalist from The News of the World (in fact it was a quantity surveyor returning home from his office in Kings Cross). Now of course he was late and he began to set up his equipment in a sort of frenzy. One of the comedians foolishly approached him to ask him to take his photograph with Henry Espadrille, as had previously been agreed with Dave. There was a brief flurry of aggressive shouts and insults before the comedian withdrew and explained to his peers that Keith was a "nutter".

The main house lights were switched off and an atmosphere of excited anticipation began to build but Mr Peel, behind his screen, was soon sinking into a state of gloom. He felt isolated and freakish and he yearned for the sound of a familiar voice. Earlier he had noticed, at the end of the bar, a payphone fixed to the wall. Why not give Caroline a call? Nobody would notice him now that most of the lights were off. His voice was his own – so in calling her he could reassure her that he was alive and well. He stood up and began to make his way to the side of the room.

****

In the house in Kent the telephone rang a few times. Mrs Peel and her son Bill had just started to eat their kedgeree and Bill suggested they let the answering machine take the call. It was bound to be either the press or one of their friends or relatives asking for news. But Mrs Peel felt instinctively that it was an important call and she moved quickly across the room and picked up the receiver.

"Hello love it's Michael" said Mr Peel.

"Michael – my God where are you? Are you alright?"

Bill stood up quickly and turned to face her, his fork still in his hand.

"I'm fine – I'm perfectly well."

"But what has happened? Where have you been?"

"I'm – it's rather complicated love but I wanted you to know that I'm fine – I don't want you to worry about me."

"Worry? I've been worried sick – we've had police dogs here looking for your corpse. Robert went berserk."

"Caroline I'm fine – it's been a hell of a thing and..."

"But Michael – please just tell me what's going on? Do you realize there's this great black man wandering around terrorising everyone we know. He was in my bedroom – he's been swigging wine with poor Aunt Alice – she thought he was you."

"The black chap is not harmful," said Mr Peel, "he's a good man – he's just been trying to help."

"Help!" said Mrs Peel with as much sarcasm as she could corral into a single word.

Bill had moved over to her and was trying to listen.

"Are you sure it's Dad?" he interrupted.

She waved her son's question away – there was no mistaking Michael's voice.

"The black chap is our friend – I promise you," continued Mr Peel. "He's got Charles Dryesdale's cheque and he's going to deposit it in our account in the morning. Then he's going to Trafalgar Square."

"But how do you know all this – are you with him?" This question silenced Mr Peel and his wife became aware of the murmuring of a crowd in the background.

"Where are you? Who are all those people talking?"

Bill took the telephone from her.

"Dad?" he asked.

"Bill – how are you dear boy?" replied his father jovially, relieved to be free of his wife's awkward question.

"Dad what's going on? Why can't you just come home?"

At this point the house lights went out completely and Dave appeared to leap onto the stage out of nowhere, to a great round of applause.

"Bill, I'll have to go," said Mr Peel quickly.

"Are you at some sort of show?" asked Bill, hearing Dave welcoming the audience through the microphone.

"I'll explain everything," said Mr Peel, realising that the call had been a mistake. "Please just tell Mum not to worry. I'm going to be fine – everything's going to get back to normal I promise." He attempted to hang up the phone but the bright stage lights served to exaggerate the near total darkness and he fumbled it. The handset dropped and swung about on its cord as Mr Peel grappled desperately for it.

On stage Dave held up the front page of the Evening Standard. "Tonight's show," he announced, "is a tribute to a new black hero." The audience instantly recognised the features of Henry Espadrille and laughed. They were familiar with the bizarre story and recognised at once that it was fertile stand-up comedy territory. "Henry Espadrille is innocent!" shouted Dave and the audience spontaneously roared their approval. Finally Mr Peel managed to grab hold of the recalcitrant receiver and return it to its cradle..

The words "Henry Espadrille is innocent," shouted through a PA system, and followed by a hearty cheer left Bill in a state of almost medical shock. He put the receiver down in silence while Mrs Peel stared at him – perceiving that something deeply unpleasant had just occurred and hardly daring to ask what it was.

Bill walked, zombie-like, back towards his kedgeree and Mrs Peel followed. They sat down and she glared fearfully at her son.

"Come on – out with it. What happened?" she finally asked.

He looked at her, feeling the need to show her the shock on his own face.

"He was at some sort of rally - for Henry Espadrille"

"What do you mean?" she asked – her imagination reeling.

"There was someone shouting about a new black hero – he said Henry Espadrille was innocent - and then there was cheering."

"Henry Espadrille?" said Mrs Peel. "But that's this bloody black man again – what in God's name was Michael doing there?"

"That wasn't Dad," said Bill. Seeing how upset his mother was he reached across and squeezed her hand.

****

Back in the Phoenix's upstairs room, Dave's introductory banter was going extremely well. His comic conceit was that Henry Espadrille was actually Michael Peel, the man he was accused of murdering. Mr Peel had been trying to go about his normal business but had been forced to invent a false name because he had turned black in the night. He was being unduly pursued as a criminal and needed only a chance to explain himself and everything would be cleared up. The audience enjoyed the absurdity of this and, as is the rule with live comedy, they found it all the funnier because it was such an up-to-the-minute current affairs story.

As Dave expanded on his theme the thought occurred to him that this comic version of events did constitute a very neat explanation for everything that had happened to the man who was concealed behind the screen. As this was the version of events that Henry (or Michael) himself had expounded he found himself wondering if it was not actually the truth. At one point he gave his head a bit of a shake to dispel this distracting thought – which threatened to throw him off his rhythm.

Once again seated behind the screen, Mr Peel felt very keenly the hopelessness of his situation. What had happened to him was so preposterous that a man was managing to make an audience laugh by simply describing it – although he had to concede that Dave did have a wonderful way with words and excellent timing. In fact after a while Mr Peel started to join in with the laughter. Now that the house lights were down the comedians seated next to him helped him fold up the screen so he could watch the show as well as hear it. He began to relax.

Dave put the other black comic on as the first act – a hugely confident young man who settled the audience in nicely. He ad-libbed some material about Henry Espadrille that expanded brilliantly on Dave's theme – claiming to be Michael Peel's son who had also turned black in the night. He had had a terrible day trying to persuade his white girlfriend to have sex with him which had ended with him shagging her senseless. At this point the girl's white father had walked in and his attempts to explain that he was actually a white boy had fallen on deaf ears and the father had chased him from the house wielding a cricket bat, which he described as "the white middle class weapon of choice." After this comic the first of the singers went on – a pretty fifteen year old called Chantelle, who warbled like a pigeon. She had a large family group in and they applauded her wildly.

The evening progressed at a merry pace. Dave returned to the Henry Espadrille theme whenever he came up to do his next intro. He managed to actually work up a certain amount of indignation about the way that Henry was being presumed to be guilty and when he announced that he was going to Trafalgar Square at noon the following day to make sure that there was no police brutality, he detected an atmosphere in the room that was conducive to a bit of rabble rousing.

"Are you with me?" he yelled and a great affirmative shout rolled back at him.

"Bollocks!" he retorted. "Saturday morning – hangovers and recriminations yes – direct political action – I don't think so."

During the interval Dave went over and checked on Mr Peel. The screen had been hastily re-erected when the house lights came up and Mr Peel was seated behind it drinking another pint of Theakstons and enjoying the banter of the comics. Dave had half expected to find that he had done a runner, disgusted to find himself the subject of so much irreverent humour. Mr Peel had felt a compulsion to leave a few times, but this was because he found the musical interludes painful on the ear. His musical tastes were restricted to material written prior to about 1954 and everything subsequent was, to him, a discordant racket. The comedy he had been enjoying heartily. In fact he was impressed by Dave's skill and his only concern was that he was going to have to follow the very sharp and amusing comics that had been on already. He had to keep reminding himself that it was all to ensure that he had a bed for the night.

"You'll be fine," reassured Dave. "They're going to be gobsmacked."

If anything the second half of the show went even better than the first. Dave began his intro by describing Michael Peel as "a Bounty bar with a heart of gold". He talked in detail about his plan to lead an army of dedicated black activists to Trafalgar Square in time for his noon appearance to ensure that Michael Peel, in his black incarnation, was not the victim of racist police brutality. "He may be white on the inside but on the outside he's one of us – and that's what counts," he yelled, but with a comical look of doubt on his face, as though he were losing track of where his loyalties really lay. "The point is," he continued, "the press will be there, the police will be there, and we can all get stuck in with some mindless argy bargy and still have time to visit the National Gallery and be home for lunch." He got the audience to chant the words "Michael Peel – black or white," before introducing the next singer, a rapper calling himself "DJ Dog Star" who was so bad even his own posse seemed to disown him and found it impossible to applaud him with real enthusiasm. It was the only bum note of the evening.

Dave got the room warmed up again quickly by announcing that the next act was the only white act of the evening and they should remember that he was not personally responsible for Britain's colonial past and the appalling depravations of the slave trade. Sensing that the room could go either way the young white comic made his way quickly to the stage and announced that he was "a black man who had turned white in the night". This got a big laugh but when he began describing how his day as a white man had gone surprisingly well this produced a couple of good laughs but then quickly petered out. He fell back on some tried and tested sex jokes and came off to hearty applause.

The last singer was a fat boy in his early twenties with a fascinating and soulful voice and a winning way of jiggling his whole body that produced whoops of delight. He had the whole audience clapping along to his song and when he finished Dave had to ignore their cries for an encore as the evening was in danger of over-running. He wrangled the audience back into line and quickly went through the highly unscientific process of judging the talent contest using a show of hands. The fat boy, who had brought the biggest mob with him, won easily.

"Ladies and Gentlemen," pronounced Dave, after the prize (an extremely cheap bottle of white wine provided by the pub) had been handed over to the beaming soul singer, "I have a great surprise for you. We've talked a good deal about the Henry Espadrille/Michael Peel story and I'm sure you've all formed your own opinions about whether he's innocent or guilty as charged. In my opinion you should reserve judgement until you have heard things from the horse's mouth. And ladies and gentlemen – the horse is here tonight…"

When he said this there was an audible gasp from the audience. Joking about Henry Espadrille was one thing – but surely a man accused of a serious crime was not going to actually appear on the stage? This was stepping over some sort of line. Dave sensed the change of mood but ploughed ahead regardless. He was not going to take Henry Espadrille off the bill now.

"So without further ado I am pleased to present to you – the man of the hour, call him Henry Espadrille, call him Michael Peel –– call him what you bloody well like – I call him a friend – I call him a legend – I call him a God – but then I do have a tendency to go over the top – he's here to cut through the lies and the libels, he's here to kick back at the knee jerk bigots – so lets big him up – because he's risked life and limb and a night in Brixton Police station to come here to our own beloved Phoenix. He's been called mentally ill - so go mad, he's been called crazy - so go stark raving bonkers. Ladies and gentlemen – I give you – Mr Henry Espadrille!"

Dave put so much energy into his introduction that the audience, though in a state of mild shock, did manage to produce some applause (greatly augmented by the three comics at the back), but it was ragged and it ran out long before Mr Peel reached the stage. Consequently he stepped up onto the slightly raised boards to resounding silence, and being unused to using a microphone stand and performing under a spotlight he spent a few awkward moments adjusting the height of the stand and getting his bearings while managing to generate some ear-splitting feedback.

The audience daren't move a muscle. They were staring with disbelief at the man they had seen that very day on the front cover of their newspaper or on the evening news – a man who was probably suffering from severe mental illness and who was suspected of murdering a pensioner. A man at whose expense they had been howling with laughter all evening.

Mr Peel peered into the dark, squinting at the blinding light as the silence deepened around him.

"Good evening." he said, finally, only to be met with more silence.

"Just to clear up any confusion – my name is Michael Peel." If anything this caused the silence to deepen, as though the audience were no longer breathing. Things were going so badly that Mr Peel searched for Dave who was seated at the edge of the front row. But when his eyes fell on Dave in the gloom he found him enthusiastically alternating between two gestures – a pair of thumbs up and a pair of rotating index fingers, to indicate that it was going well and he should carry on.

"I would like to reassure you first of all by saying – I haven't killed anyone.
The nearest I ever came was Christmas shopping in Debenhams."

This produced loud laughter from Dave and the three comedians at the back – and a nervous titter from the audience.

"The truth is that until about seven thirty this morning I was living a fairly uneventful sort of existence. I run a small PR firm, I like to do the Telegraph crossword…" He suddenly felt as though he were staring into an empty abyss. Was his life so boring?

"I have an interest in Lepidoptera - moths." He went on – suddenly confident of his subject. "In fact last summer I went on a moth hunting trip to the Bukk National Park in Hungary. I saw some fabulous species – the dusky clearwing – fascinating micro moth that looks like a small wasp, the…er…scarce vapourer – um…" His mind was blank again. He glared madly out into the dark, straining to see if the audience were listening – or even there.

"The three humped prominent!" he suddenly shouted into the silence, startling the audience and then producing a hearty laugh. The truth was his impersonation of an old-world white public school eccentric who happened to be the wrong colour was pitch perfect and they were loving it.

"But this is not a moth lecture," he went on, "I'm here to tell you what happened today. This morning I was lying in bed – thinking over my plans for the day – a very important day in my business year as a matter of fact - when my wife Caroline entered the bedroom. Now she knows me well, we've been married for forty-two years – but she took one look at me and started screaming hysterically. It was not until I had gone into the bathroom and seen myself in the mirror that I understood why. I was born in Liskeard Community Hospital in 1945 to white Caucasian parents. I was a white baby, a white boy, and I have been a white man for the vast majority of my adult life."

Again there was laughter – now more general, and somewhat mocking in nature. Mr Peel waited for the noise to subside.

"But what I saw in the mirror was a black man."

At the back of the room Keith had the video camera purring away on 'record', locked off on the tripod and framed up in a wide-to-mid shot so that Henry Espadrille could not wander off camera. This allowed him to snap away with his stills camera. He had no need of a flash due to the bright stage lights but when he saw a well-dressed middle-aged black woman (the mother of one of the singers) taking a small camera from her handbag he leaned over her menacingly and whispered "No photographs of Mr Espadrille" with considerable menace, directly into her face. She froze, traumatized more by his bad breath than his words, and slipped the camera back into her bag.

On stage Mr Peel ploughed on. His eyes had adjusted to the lighting and he could make out the expressions of the first few rows of spectators. Their eyes were glinting with a mixture of fascination and amusement – but there was something hostile in the atmosphere.

"I have to say that my day as a black man has not been an easy one," he said, deciding to show a bit of empathy to his fellow people of colour. The comment produced a general wave of laughter.

".. and if it is in any way typical of the day-to-day experience of black people in this country then I can assure you that you have my complete sympathy."

Boom! A wave of laughter hit him, causing him to lose his bearings for a moment. What exactly was so funny about that?

"Clearly, however, my peculiar circumstance has contributed to the unpleasantness. I am fairly sure, and I certainly hope, that the police are not called every time you visit your family doctor."

Instead of laughter this produced a sort of perplexed silence. Much to Mr Peel's surprise, a man of Caribbean origin (in fact the father of the first singer) piped up with a question.

"What you see the doctor for then?" he asked.

Mr Peel took a moment to adjust to this new development – during which he searched for the man in the audience. He found him looking back at him with good- natured curiosity.

"I went to the doctor to try to find out why I had turned into a black man."

"It's not an illness you know," the man shot back, without hesitation triggering a hearty laugh. Had Mr Peel been looking at Dave at this point he would have seen him wince.

"That was pretty much what my doctor said," replied Mr Peel – unfortunately producing not laughter but more silence. Dave now winced again while mouthing the word "fuck". To allow a heckler to be funny was one thing, to then come back with a dead line meant you were now standing with your neck in a noose. What was worse the audience seemed to really think he had been to see a doctor and asked to be cured of his blackness.

"Black skin not good enough for you?" shouted someone else. A wave of half amused, half angry assent fanned out through the audience. Dave became alarmed and stood up. He turned to face the audience and made a calming gesture.

"Hold it folks, hold it," he said. "Let the man speak."

"You are ill, you are sick and you are insultin'," shouted someone else and the comment effected an instant mood swing in the room. It was becoming a rabble.

"You want to get along to the Maudsley," yelled a woman at the front, referring to a local hospital for the mentally ill, her voice cracking with intense passion.

"Tell them you're a white man," she went on, "they'll understand you alright darling." This got a laugh but the woman was actually in a rage and her anger now shifted to Dave. "You put a mentally ill man onto the stage! What's wrong with you, don't you know anything?"

"I'm not mentally ill!" Mr Peel almost shouted into the microphone, causing the sound to distort and another painful blast of feedback to screech through the speakers. In truth it had been a mistake for a man with a tendency to completely lose his temper to take to the public stage in such trying circumstances. He was starting to feel a tightening in his chest and the sensation of blood running rapidly to his head. Keith, who was now looking through the video camera's viewfinder, was the first to detect that something disturbing was starting to happen when he noticed that Mr Peel's eyes had become bloodshot. "I challenge any one in this room to point out one insane thing I have done today."

"You got out of bed," sniped a voice from the edge of the room – prompting a hearty laugh.

"Why have you got to be this posh man anyway?" asked the Caribbean father. "You think you're Trevor McDonald or something?" This produced another gale of laughter and Mr Peel felt an awful sting of humiliation, the like of which he had not known since he had been debagged at school and thrown into a bank of nettles. He felt dizzy and reckless.

"You want me to start pretending to be a black man?" he asked furiously, now beyond the point of no return and actually perceiving a red mist. "What am I supposed to do - start rolling my eyes and doing a savage dance?"

He had lost control of himself – and had he possessed a fire poker he would almost certainly have destroyed a porcelain King Charles spaniel, had one been available. As it was, no obvious opportunity for mindless destruction presented itself.

Instead the words to a song, from the first James Bond film 'Dr. No' (which he had seen probably twenty times in his life) sprung to his mind fully formed and he made the spontaneous, and ill-advised, decision to sing it. He had hoped that the audience would give him a chance to tell his tale and demonstrate, beyond any doubt, who he was. Instead they were bating him like a bear. Well he'd show the ungrateful buggers.

"Underneath de mango tree, me honey and me," he began to sing, and as he did he performed a strange little dipping dance that took him left and right across the stage. He mistook the silence that this produced as an indication that he had retaken control of the room – but in fact he had brutally offended almost everyone (the three comics excepted – they collapsed with helpless laughter, physically supporting each other in their chairs).

Dave made the decision to curtail the performance. He walked up to Mr Peel and took him by the elbow.

"I think that will probably do us," he said but Mr Peel still held the microphone and his little song and dance had built up a momentum of its own. Members of the audience were standing up. Dave made a grab for the microphone but Mr Peel whisked it away and sang on until he could no longer remember the words.

"I intend to keep my promise to hand myself in to the authorities at Trafalgar Square at noon," he announced, by way of conclusion, "and welcome any support you might care to give me." This was met with a tidal wave of booing and one furious shout of

"Fuck off". It was only now that Mr Peel realised that he was in trouble. He looked across in alarm at Dave, who managed to convey a great deal of information by simply holding out his hand while wearing an expression of deep regret. Mr Peel handed him the microphone. Keith, sensing that the real meat of the evening had been committed to film and video, sloped across to the payphone – ready now to reveal his whereabouts to his media contacts.

"Ladies and gents – I promised you controversy," proclaimed Dave, greatly relieved to be back in control of the amplified sound. His statement was punctuated by a ball of paper that arced through the air and bounced off Mr Peel's head. "The fan mail's arriving already," quipped Dave who suddenly found that several people were standing in front of him, angrily berating him for his bad taste and misjudgement. He brought the show to an abrupt end with a "Thank you and goodnight."

Outside the Phoenix two motorcycle couriers waited, the result of Keith's telephone call. Absurdly they were soon joined by an ambulance. It had been summonsed, somewhat impractically, by the woman who had made the comment about the Maudsley hospital. In fact Dave and Mr Peel passed the medics in the doorway and Dave directed them upstairs, saying that they couldn't miss the patient as he was "The one claiming to be Napoleon and frothing at the mouth." He then took Mr Peel down a side street and into the waiting room of a mini cab company he occasionally used when he was feeling flush after a good turnout at the Phoenix. Back at the pub Keith handed over a video tape to one courier and a roll of film to the other – and took receipt of a couple of pleasingly fat envelopes. With Keith it was cash up front or you could go hang yourself.

****

In the taxi Dave delivered complex instructions to the driver on how to get to his flat while Mr Peel sat quietly – enjoying the relative peace of the car's muffled interior. He reflected that Dave was rather a fine chap.

"I am sorry," he said simply, after Dave had settled back into his seat.

"About what?" asked Dave, genuinely unsure of what he was talking about.

"My little singsong was inappropriate – offensive even."

Dave glanced at him, a glint in his eye, enjoying the understatement.

"Well as an act it is a bit on the offensive side in its current form – but with a bit of work…"

"I'm not actually planning to enter show business."

"Shame," said Dave, "I think you've got something there."

"What do you mean?"

"I'm thinking - a black man who pretends to be a posh white man – could be a funny way to explore the thorny old issue of race. I'd give it a go myself but I'm not really into character stuff."

"But the audience nearly rioted."

"As they did at the first performance of 'The Rite of Spring" as I recall." Said Dave with deliberate nonchalance.

"Do you mean the ballet?" replied Mr. Peel, failing to hide his surprise at the man's erudition.

"I do indeed mean the ballet my friend but its all show business isn't it? Look my point is that you got a reaction. The act is crude but with work you might have something. Worth thinking about if you're looking for a new career."

The thought plunged Mr Peel into silence. As a creature he was not particularly suited to change. He had worked in the same industry all his life, bought all his suits from The Savoy Tailor's Guild and had all his hair cuts at a place on The Strand. Of course one had to adapt a bit. In recent years he and Caroline had been quietly curtailing their lifestyle. For all the great changes in the world - improvements in healthcare, communications and transport - the only discernible effect on himself was a gradual and remorseless reduction in his income. They no longer took a winter holiday and had stopped going out for expensive dinners. This had all been done with the minimum of fuss and he sometimes felt that the simpler life suited them rather well. His transformation into a black man was, however, a change that he was clearly ill suited to. The whole thing had been accompanied, from the very beginning, by hysteria, excitable mobs and the flashing lights of emergency vehicles. He would not, as a white man, have been averse to the idea of a late entry into the world of show business, in fact he would have been flattered at the suggestion, but to become a black character comedian who pretended to be a white man, making fun of his own trying predicament - frankly it was too much of a stretch. The very thought of it made him long for the certainties of a police interview and a prison cell.

Dave's flat consisted of the top floor of a Victorian terraced house. After squeezing past a bicycle in the hallway they climbed a narrow set of stairs as Dave explained that his girlfriend and his little boy would be there so they needed to be a bit quiet. Mr Peel was alarmed by this news and he asked if he was expected.

"Best to spring these things on the missus frankly – that way she can't say no."

The door opened directly into a small living room with a kitchenette attached. Dave's girlfriend was sitting drowsily watching a video when they entered.

"Hello love - I've picked up a stray performer for the night," explained Dave.

"This is Michael. Michael – Debs."

"Hello Michael what can I get you?" she asked as she got to her feet and shook his hand, smiling warmly.

"Please don't get up," said Mr Peel, experiencing some embarrassment as she tightened the belt on her dressing gown. "I do apologise for imposing on you like this."

Debs took a moment to acknowledge his old-school Englishness – which she did by raising her eyebrows and glancing at Dave.

"You're a very decent sort – letting Dave bring waifs and strays in at all hours," continued Mr Peel.

"Well, you're hardly that are you," said Debs, admiring his suit. "You're very welcome here. Dave will be getting it in the neck later but that's just for not warning me."

They sat around a little table chatting over a pot of tea. Debs' life was extremely hectic. She worked as a nurse on an A&E ward and she had only just come off shift. Her mother had been taking care of Byron, their little boy, until Debs had returned to the flat just an hour before. They were all tired but laughter came easily. After a while Byron, a five year old boy, wandered sleepily into the room complaining that he couldn't sleep. Although Debs pretended to be annoyed she allowed him to sit on her lap for a while so she could show her son off to their visitor. As they talked about the little boy's progress at school Mr Peel realised that he could not think of anyone he knew in London who would allow him to stay the night at such short notice with so little fuss. These people, to whom he was essentially a complete stranger, had welcomed him into their home and were now treating him like a trusted friend. He was touched. At one point Dave winked at Mr Peel, as though to say: "Things have worked out pretty well haven't they." Although Debs was looking away at the time she saw the wink out of the corner of her eye and filed it away for later examination.

Byron finally agreed to go back to sleep after Dave had promised to take him to Trafalgar Square the next day. Debs carried him to his room and Dave asked Mr Peel to help him with the sofa bed. Once he had been shown where the bathroom was and had been thoroughly assured that he should make himself at home, Mr Peel put on an extra large "Phoenix Talent Night" T-shirt, brushed his teeth with a brand new Thomas the Tank Engine toothbrush and went to bed.

The previous night, across town in a little know district of London called Sands End, just south west of Chelsea Harbour, a sequence of events were set in motion that were to knock the British tabloid press slightly off-kilter, leaving them with a sharp and urgent appetite for a good front-page story – an appetite that was to impact considerably on the degree to which the general public would be caught up in the saga of Henry Espadrille.

A young man who was a member of the British royal family, in fact no less than a cousin of the Queen (who we shall refer to henceforth as The Royal Youth) was enjoying a night out with his girlfriend at a house he had never before visited. The house belonged to an old university friend of his girlfriend but there was a spontaneity to the evening which left no time to vet or reflect on the rather random set of people who found themselves sitting around a table with a cousin of the Monarch. Nevertheless they had a jolly old time, drank a great deal of wine and then moved on to shots of flavoured vodka to thoroughly wash down the rainbow trout cooked in white wine and almonds. It was such an amusing and convivial evening that The Royal Youth broke a personal rule and allowed himself to be persuaded to partake of a joint that was being passed around the table. This first joint was smoked without much comment but it signalled to a somewhat venal and duplicitous young man called Adrian, a tenant in the house who worked as an estate agent, that The Royal Youth was really letting his hair down. After more vodka shots had been downed the atmosphere became positively bacchanalian and the party entered into such hilarious high jinks as strip charades, Guinness and Famous Grouse depth charges, a game played with a burnt cork called 'Ibble Dibble,' which left The Royal Youth with two soot marks scrawled on his cheeks, and finally a riotous contest, invented on the spot and Christened "Knockdown Polo," which involved the girls (with their tops removed) getting on their boyfriend's shoulders and attempting to dismount each other during reckless charges across the dining room, while yelling "Giddy up fucker!" and other wild cries of encouragement. During this game Adrian, who did not have a girlfriend and felt left out, started taking photographs. While leaning disconsolately against the sideboard he had stumbled on one of the newly invented 'disposable' cameras in a WH Smith's bag. At first he pretended to be greatly interested in it, but when nobody commented he started snapping away. He had remained relatively sober and he quickly observed that even the crude flash of the little plastic camera did not seem to alert people to what he was doing. When everyone settled down for a rest another large joint was rolled and, to cut a long story short, Adrian snapped a photograph of The Royal Youth taking a puff.

In the cold light of dawn Adrian reflected on what he had in his possession: an undeveloped roll of film containing pictures of a young man in close and direct line to the throne playing 'Knockdown Polo' with a girl on his shoulders and a single snap of him smoking a marijuana joint. The Knockdown Polo pictures would clearly liven up the pages of any tabloid. Unfortunately the girl was wearing a bra, which stratospherically reduced its value, but his snap of an authentic top-of-the-range blueblood puffing on a joint was clearly a very hot piece of property indeed. He knew this because he was interested in money – always had been and always would be. A royal personage partaking of an illegal narcotic took the story of the British Royal Family forward into new territory. It said something fresh about the state of things. It was a picture, he calculated, that was potentially worth the kind of money that allowed you to start buying and selling property independently – possibly even that nice little two up two down on Stephendale Road that was going for £175,000. Life changing money. Money, he concluded, for which he was prepared to trade in his frankly rather flimsy friendship with the other occupants of the house, who all lay vilely hung over in their beds as he plotted.

Adrian went to work as usual but at lunchtime he set up his headquarters in a pub on The Kings Road where he requisitioned the payphone, placed a stack of ten and fifty pence pieces on the nearest table and called the tabloids, insisting in each case that he speak to the editor. The editors, none of whom had got where they were by being pushovers, each in turn played it cool while secretly experiencing the very thrills that had lured them into the newspaper business in the first place. It had been a slow news day with only tedious political wranglings and the usual swarm of press releases to fill pages. The Henry Espadrille story was good value but the Evening Standard published the pictures from the Dryesdale press conference in their first, and subsequent, editions and without the oxygen of fresh photographic material the story's vitality was rapidly waning. It was hard to see how it could earn its place on the front page of the Saturday editions. The price for the picture of The Royal Youth crept up, although not to quite the levels that Adrian had allowed his fevered imagination to conjur up. By 4 p.m. he was being offered £4750 and he closed the deal. He returned to the house, scene of the previous night's revelries, and drew himself a bath. He had one foot in it when the doorbell rang.

On his doorstep was a very rarefied creature indeed. A young Eton and Cambridge educated toff who was deep into the "second six" of his Barrister's pupillage. Resplendent in his Saville Row suit and with the air of a man undertaking a menial task that was both beneath him and at the same time extremely important, he thrust an envelope at Adrian who, dazzled by the magnificence of the creature before him (he had a sense that the man's very shoelaces were made of silk) took it.

This dazzling emissary was a 'pupil' of The Queen of England's personal legal adviser, who had been alerted to the incriminating photographs of his client's cousin by one of the unsuccessful editors in the bidding war for the pictures. His boss was paid extremely handsomely to deal with just this kind of thing and he had acted swiftly and expertly. A few astonishingly perspicacious telephone calls established that the disposable camera did not belong to the disgraceful young man who was trying to sell the pictures and his 'pupil' was dispatched to deliver an injunction into the hands of Adrian with swift and brutal efficiency. Every editor on what had, until a few years before, been termed 'Fleet Street,' was quickly informed that the vendor did not own the copyright in the pictures he was attempting to sell and the story was dead before it ever got to poke its disreputable little head into the great blaze of the public's gaze.

This all left the editors of Britain's colourful tabloids in a bit of a state. They had been stirred up by a great story, had viciously tried to outbid each other, had put all their chief journalists onto the story – on the publications without the pictures they were tasked with working on spoilers – then someone had 'betrayed' the whole thing to an old enemy (The Queen's lawyer) and now they had great gaping holes where their front pages should be. It was into this void that the ripe fruit of Henry Espadrille's Phoenix Talent night performance dropped. The photo agency that had bought Keith's undeveloped roll of film for a mere £2350 (the best deal they ever did) knew its business. Rather than offer an exclusive and get bogged down in a lengthy auction that might well have resulted in missing the looming print deadlines, the pictures were offered at a flat rate of £35,000 and every national paper (including the Daily Sport) bought them willingly and with relief. The videotape of the evening's performance did not arrive at the BBC in time for The

News at Ten but was digested by news editors through the night. The material made its first appearance on an early morning Greater London Radio news bulletin where its impact was reduced by the lack of visual stimulus but by 8 a.m. Henry Espadrille was dancing "Underneath the mango tree" on those of the nation's Saturday morning television screens that were switched to the BBC news.

When Debs got up at eight Mr Peel was already in the bathroom having a shave. He felt that, although his ordeal was far from over, he was close to banking his cheque, the only outcome that he had some control over and one that would make life a great deal easier for his wife in the coming weeks of unavoidable confusion over his identity. Consequently he was humming quite happily to himself when he heard the telephone ring.

The call was from Deb's great but excitable friend Angie, a fellow nurse, whose radio alarm had gone off at eight so that she had awoken to the sound of a newsreader talking about Henry Espadrille's appearance at the Phoenix Talent Night. She immediately called Debs and began squealing inarticulately about how Dave was "All over the radio news," and had "really gone and bloody done it this time." Debs tried to get her to calm down and deliver one useful informative sentence. "Just tell me," she said, "What's going on."

"Henry Espadrille was at Dave's night – why didn't you tell me?"

"Who's Henry Espadrille when he's at home?" Asked Debs, whose shift the day before had been far too hectic to allow time for reading the Evening Standard.

"Where you been woman?" countered Angela "He's the one wanted for killing that bloke – whatisname – Michael Peel - the one he was pretending to be last night at Dave's show!" Debs froze. She wanted to hang up but her limbs were not cooperating. Angie babbled on. "Why didn't you tell me you silly cow! I'd have come to that – bit of edge, bit of danger. A wanted man in the flesh. Geoff says it's in all the papers too…"

Debs managed to regain mastery of her arms and hung up.

She was barely any wiser about what was going on. The key words for her were "killing" and "wanted man" and they referred, as far as she could tell, to the man sleeping in her spare bed. If there was one thing likely to inflame the ire of Debs it was the idea that her son might be exposed to criminality. As the mother of a black boy being raised in inner city London she was well aware of the statistics. Byron was a fine boy and she was making damned sure he was well educated. Stopping him from being dragged down by evil influences required constant and fierce vigilance. Now his own father had brought a criminal into their home. She again recalled Dave's wink of the evening before and saw it in a new and sinister light.

She strode purposefully down the little corridor towards the bedroom she shared with Dave, inside which he was sleeping the sleep of the tired and innocent. She paused on seeing Mr Peel's suit on a hanger on the handle of the bathroom door. She could not resist searching the pockets and quickly found Michael Peel's cheque for £12,000. This was a large amount of money and it felt wrong that it was lying loose in a pocket. What was it that Angie had said? "The one he was pretending to be."At this moment she was startled by a sudden shout of "bugger" coming from the bathroom and she felt a fresh wave of fury. To the list of things that Dave had exposed Byron to could now be added offensive language. She strode into Byron's room and started to get him dressed.

Mr Peel had decided to take a quick shower and after a momentary scorching (which produced the shout of "bugger") he had soothing hot water blasting down on him. After he had banked his check he would be able to hand his problems over to professionals. Whatever they made of him – whether it be criminal, lunatic, or medical oddity – working out what to do with him would be their headache, not his. As he showered, humming the tune to "Underneath the Mango tree" (which seemed to have become indelibly implanted in his head) Debs bustled out of the flat with a complaining Byron. Understandably the boy wanted some breakfast but Debs was determined to get him out of the building until she had established what, if any, threat her houseguest posed to his wellbeing. As it happened she did not have to go far to find the information she needed. Mrs Jacks, her downstairs neighbour, a nervous elderly woman who had not left her home for two days, was a subscriber to the Daily Mirror and the new edition lay neatly folded on the door mat. Cradling Byron in one arm she managed to unfold the paper and found herself staring at the face of the fugitive

Henry Espadrille. As Byron whined about Coco Pops she apprised herself of the whole sorry saga.

Dave had had some rude awakenings in his life but never before had he been awoken by strangulation. With one hand Debs pressed down on his windpipe, while with the other she held the cheque in front of his startled eyes.

"You fucking cretin!" she spat furiously. "Bringing a murderer into our home!" Dave attempted to speak but he had breathed out just before she struck. He struggled desperately and she allowed him to breath once before re-tightening her grip.

"I'm taking Byron to Nana's," she said. "You just get that man out of this house. We have some serious talking to do."

She released him and walked immediately out the door and into Byron's little box room off the corridor where she packed a small bag. Dave rolled over in bed, grasping at his throat and coughing and spluttering. In his mind he reached back to what he now saw was the decisive moment in all this – the moment, back in the pub the evening before, when he had thought to himself; "I am the man of the house and I have a duty to make it in show business." It was then that he had sealed his fate. His next thought was that Debs was threatening to disappear with Mr Peel's cheque and this was fundamentally wrong. He threw on his clothes.

Mr Peel heard the commotion and switched off the shower. The little boy was whimpering – something about Pop Tarts - and this was followed by heavy footfalls in the little corridor. Further away someone appeared to be choking. Could his hogging of the bathroom have offended these people in some fundamental way? Maybe they were more different than he had supposed. He hastily dried himself then silently cursed when he remembered he had hung his clothes outside the door. Now he would have to open the door while wrapped only in a towel. He undid the lock and opened the door fractionally. He peeped through and found the corridor empty. He stepped out.

At this moment Dave came charging out of the bedroom. He ignored Mr Peel but glanced instead into Byron's box room. Finding it empty he headed swiftly down the corridor towards the flat's exit.

"Is anything wrong?" asked Mr Peel.

"You could put it that way," replied Dave. "She's run off with your cheque."

With this horrendous statement he was gone – and an electrical storm seemed to erupt in Mr Peel's brain. He flung himself towards the exit catching the towel on the door handle in the process. He ripped madly at it but it would not come loose so he flung it aside.

"What do you mean she's got my cheque?" he shouted as he ran naked down the stairs. Dave already had the door onto the street open and he glanced back only momentarily before running outside. He would have spoken but the sight of the naked Mr Peel robbed him of the power of speech.

"You've got to get it back!" shouted Mr Peel.

The door at the top of the stairs had swung shut behind Mr Peel but so focused was he on the whereabouts of his cheque that the significance of this did not immediately dawn on him. In fact he was barely even conscious of his nudity until he was standing looking out into the street where he saw Dave sprinting after a black cab that had just pulled away from the curb. A sudden gust of wind made Mr Peel acutely aware that he had no clothes on and he acknowledged that, naked, he could do nothing. He ran back up the stairs and found the door to the flat firmly locked.

Mr Peel had shouted the word "bugger" a good few times in his life – it was his serious swearword of choice – the big gun, as it were, reserved for those occasions when he smashed his thumb with a hammer or scorched his body with an ill-tuned power shower. Up until now the loudest he had ever shouted it was when he had been opening a bottle of wine with an unusual opener given to him as a present by his son Bill as a birthday present. It worked by pumping air into the bottle until it forced the cork out from inside. He had been using it at a dinner party at home and the bottle had exploded with such violence that red wine had been sprayed evenly over their pristine white tablecloth and pretty much every guest in the room. Mr Peel got a nasty cut on his hand and Caroline had almost fainted with embarrassment. The volume of his colossal shout of "bugger!" had become a minor legend in the neighbourhood.

On finding that he was a naked prisoner of the narrow stairway and hallway he didn't so much shout the word now, as howl it like a wolf. Downstairs Mrs Jacks froze as she watered her aspidistra and felt a fear she hadn't experienced since the Blitz. The hairs bristled on the back of her neck and she found herself muttering a prayer for deliverance.

***

Dave's pleas to Debs as her taxi pulled away up Kennington Road had fallen on deaf ears. It was not easy to explain the intricacies of bank regulations as regards crossed cheques to an angry woman of Nigerian descent who believed you had compromised her son's future. He soon found himself standing alone on the street yelling pointlessly as the taxi vanished around a corner.

He made the decision then and there to give up. He had involved himself with this Henry Espadrille character long enough and now it had caused one of those perennial rifts with his girlfriend that were such a colossal pain and cost so much in dignity and flowers to repair. He turned with the intention of going back to the flat and giving his guest the sad news that he would not be banking his Coutts & Co. cheque that morning – when, like the U.S. Cavalry pouring over a hill, a pristine black cab with its cheerful yellow light glowing, loomed into view. Without thinking he raised his hand and hailed it.

***

The naked Mr Peel sat on the stairs hugging his shoulders and telling himself that the situation was not as dire as it seemed. Dave would be back at any moment and he would soon be able to get dressed and be on his way. The cheque was perhaps now lost – but all problems were relative. The relief of being out of this chilly corridor, with the ever-present threat that someone from the downstairs flat might appear, would surely compensate for other disappointments. The worst thing about his predicament was that there seemed to be a cold draft actually rising through the stairway, as though there were some open aperture inside the structure, and as he was not yet even fully dry he began to worry that he might catch a serious chill. He tried moving down into the hall at the bottom of the stairs where it was warmer – but he was now standing naked by the door of the downstairs flat.

In the hallway stood the bicycle that he and Dave had squeezed past the evening before – a mountain bike that Dave had bought in a Halford's sale and barely used. Mr Peel tried squatting behind this bike but as a means of covering his nudity it was useless and it was extremely uncomfortable to squat against the cold wall.

He finally found himself seated on the bicycle itself, toying nervously with its little bell and staring at the front door – willing Dave to return and end his purgatory.

***

Dave's taxi caught up with Debs' at a set of traffic lights.

"Debs sweetheart – please listen to me," he called out through his open window in his most reasonable and contrite voice. Debs' window quickly unwound and her angry head thrust out at him. He decided to get his bid in before she could work herself up into even more of a rage.

"The only people who can benefit from that cheque are Michael Peel and his wife – they are going to lose their house if it isn't banked."

"Why do you care so much about these people?" she demanded, "your number one priority is Byron – you let that take second place to this…"

"Debs – darling - this is too complicated to be explained at a traffic light." he interrupted. "Please just give me the cheque". He thrust out his hand and the light turned amber. The two taxi drivers gunned their accelerators – and moved in tandem for just long enough for Debs to be able to hand Dave the cheque with a colossal gesture of disgust.

***

Mrs Jacks was aware that there was a presence outside her door. She could hear the sinister and repetitive tinkling of a little bell and sensed that whatever it was it was connected with the vulgar and unearthly howl that had so rattled her before. She desperately wanted to call the police but she needed more information. Bells and swearing were, in this day and age, insufficient disturbances to bring the officers of the law rushing to your aid. For some time she stood at her door, alert for any sound, keen to get her hands on her one luxury – her Daily Mirror. There was just the tinkling – and, she felt sure, the sound of a man occasionally sighing. Dare she look? She raised her hand to the door handle – barely daring to breathe. The door, she knew, could not be opened silently. Would she have time to open it and look, then shut it again before the unknown menace overpowered her? She simply could not resist looking, even though she felt that she was doing something stupid. Her life had become so dull that a part of her even welcomed the thought of a terrible drama.

Perhaps she would escape with two black eyes and her picture in the Kennington Advertiser. A bit of attention – a bit of old fashioned sympathy - would be frankly welcome.

She opened the door a crack and the full obscenity was revealed - a large naked middle aged Negro astride a bicycle in her hallway. Nothing had prepared her for this and her reflexes failed her. Instead of shutting the door she remained rooted to the spot and her jaw flopped open. Finally a quavering high pitched wailing sound erupted from her throat.

Moments before Mrs Jacks started wailing, Mr Peel's own alert senses picked up hints that Dave was returning. He heard the humming of a taxi, a door opening and the sound of banter between the driver and his customer. Yes, it was Dave's voice. Mr Peel was about to open the door when a hideous wailing sound assaulted his left ear and he saw the old lady standing in her doorway, her mouth wide open like the gaping top of an old sock hanging on a nail. He walked the bicycle to the front door and opened it – desperate to get Dave into the hallway where he could explain everything. The taxi was just pulling away and Dave was putting his wallet back into his jeans pocket. Seeing Mr Peel seated naked on his bicycle with old Mrs Jacks standing in her doorway, crying out like an expiring octogenarian banshee, Dave immediately understood that the poor man had been trapped naked in the corridor. Anxious to assuage his suffering with some good news he pulled out the cheque and waved it at him from the pavement.

Kenny Mbu, a fifteen year old from the local council estate, wearing the uniform of his gang (navy Nike hoodie, black tracksuit bottoms, Nike trainers) was at that moment flitting along the nearby pavement on his low saddled BMX stunt bike. He knew Dave and they had an established tradition of lively insults, exchanged as they occasionally passed each other on the street. Dave would call him a delinquent, a statistic waiting to happen, and a hundred other epithets and Kenny, who knew about Dave's night-time occupation, would call him "funny man" or "Mr Comedian," and would demand that he tell him a joke. Seeing Dave waving what looked like a cheque was too good an opportunity to miss. If he was, as Dave so often pointed out, a teenage criminal, then should he not be true to this character and whip this cheque out of his hand?

"Hey Mr Comedian – thanks for that," he quipped and the cheque vanished from Dave's grip.

When Mr Peel witnessed this development a transformation took place. He realised that he was not a financial PR man approaching retirement who was trying to get himself out of a bit of a fix. He was an officer of the Royal Marines and he was at war – stuck behind enemy lines and fighting for his life. Yes he was naked, yes he had not ridden a bicycle for twenty-five years but only one thing mattered and that was victory. He launched himself into the street.

"Oi – bring that back you little bastard!" shouted Dave at the swiftly departing youth – a comment that only served to harden Kenny Mbu's attitude. Dave now saw Mr Peel flash naked past him on the bicycle and his heart was gripped with a panic he had not known since he once lost control of an audience at a gig in Harlesden. This was not just very bad – it was flamboyantly horrendous.

"Don't do that!" he shouted, "Michael – anything but that – please – I'll give you the money myself – I'll work nights for a year!" He roared, but his cries fell on deaf ears and he soon found himself quietly mumbling to himself. "Not naked cycling Michael – please – not naked cycling in Kennington…"

Mr Peel had the hooded figure in his sights. The boy seemed to be riding a very strange contraption – the saddle was so low it looked as though it had been set wrongly or belonged to a child. The wheels also seemed to be quite small. Although Mr Peel was cycling unsteadily, he was actually gaining on his prey. But Kenny was not yet aware that he was being pursued and was taken up with the business of examining a cheque for £12,000. This was a colossal amount of money. That comedy geezer would be well mad. He would make him stew a bit longer – just for a lark. Probably take a turn through the estate and back onto Kennington Road where he was sure to find Mr Comedian hopping about like a rat on a hotplate.

It was at this moment that Kenny's instincts prickled – alerting him to danger. Something was behind him. He turned and saw it – a demon bearing down on him. At least it looked like a demon. Just as the first people to be attacked by soldiers on horseback mistook them for supernatural beings, Kenny misread the out-of-place nudity of the middle aged black man on the mountain bike and was convinced that some agent of hell had been unleashed to punish him.

He veered sharply to the right and entered his estate – his home turf. It was a place of many steps and railings, low walls and steep little banks of grass worn to bare patches by the tread of feet and the toxic effects of concentrated dog shit. It was the very arena in which Kenny had learned the skills of the BMX stunt rider. Terrified though he was, it occurred to him that his whole life had probably been leading up to this moment.

Mr Peel felt a surge of euphoria as he too steered sharply to the right and entered the estate. Maybe it was the feeling of having committed utterly to a course of action that was outrageously bold – or just the freezing air on his body – but he had never before felt so alive. All of his frustrations – the immense shelving pile of irritations and disappointments built up over a life time were now concentrated into the infuriating hooded figure frantically pedalling away and hunched over his handle bars in front of him. The little sod with his cheque.

The chase took on a distinct character. While Kenny went straight at any object and either jumped it, slid across it or skidded around it, the naked Mr Peel barrelled along the main disabled access path, the longest and most circuitous route. Although this meant that Kenny was quickly far ahead of his pursuer he was also in constant danger of taking a tumble as he ran through the entire gamut of stunts at his disposal. It was, however, Mr Peel who suffered the first fall – and it was a spectacular one.

The disabled path was not designed for speed. Several times it backed onto itself as it climbed feebly upwards. Mr Peel was not so deranged as to attempt any flying stunts – he had only just got to grips with the gears, but he made the rash decision to cycle down a flight of steps in order to make up lost time. He hesitated only momentarily, then rattled madly downwards, standing on the pedals and flexing his knees to absorb the shock. But he gained speed at a terrifying rate and he realised too late that he was out of control. When he arrived at the bottom he was travelling too fast to avoid a large concrete and pebbledash shrubbery and his front wheel slammed into it, sending him flying spectacularly over the handlebars. He landed on his back on top of a mangy privet hedge.

Kenny saw the demon – who, he now realised, was just a mentally ill person - shooting down the flight of stairs and it gave him the impetus to try his most outrageous stunt yet. He leaped onto the flat paving stones that topped a low sloping wall and sped to where his gang had built a jump that, in ideal conditions, sent you flying over a chain link fence and into a small park. Several of his friends had succeeded in making this jump and Kenny had been building up to it. Now he was going to go for it.

What defeated Kenny, however, was the fact that just before he launched himself he saw the lunatic's crash out of the corner of his eye and it distracted him. This momentary loss of concentration translated into a lack of commitment at the crucial moment. He cleared the fence but the back wheel caught the top of it, causing Kenny and the bike to jerk violently downwards and slamming him into the pavement on the other side. Only his youth and an instinctive body roll saved him from serious injury. He escaped with a badly sprained wrist and a violent blow to his left testicle.

Mr Peel rose naked from the privet hedge. He was scratched and bruised – but his determination was intact. He saw that the hooded delinquent had also fallen and he took off across the dreary urban space that separated them.

The pursuit of Kenny through the large estate had not gone unnoticed. A mother returning from the shops with three children had screamed quite early on, and a group of three elderly men had watched the naked Mr Peel swish past them – only to wonder if they had just dreamed it. Up on the balconies of the estate itself, one of Kenny's 'bloods' had just sleepily exited his flat to smoke a ciggie when he looked down and saw Kenny skipping and pirouetting his way swiftly across the terrain below on his bike. At first he watched with sleepy admiration but when he saw a large nude man pursuing him he wasted no time in stirring up the rest of the posse, who all lived on the estate.

Kenny was still on the ground clutching his groin when he became aware that his pursuer was clambering over the fence. Mr Peel was panting and sweating like a racehorse – but there was so much adrenalin in his veins that he felt he could leap over a building (if his heart didn't pack up first).

"Please boss," whimpered Kenny, whose courage had failed him. He felt a keen sense of unfairness. He was not a coward and had handled himself well enough in the past but total nudity in an assailant suggested terrifying levels of insanity, and the horrendous agony in his left nut had collapsed what little will remained to put up a fight.

"Just give me my cheque," ordered Mr Peel and Kenny reached inside his hoodie pocket where he had stuffed it. He held it out and Mr Peel snatched it back, glancing at it to be sure it really was Charles Dryesdale's cheque. What a remarkably exotic object it suddenly seemed in these surroundings. The elegant calligraphy of the Coutts & Co. logo seemed to wake him from a dream and he was suddenly, brutally, aware of his nudity.

What is more, he now realised that people – young black people – were approaching. They all wore the same clothes as the thief who was writhing at his feet and they did not look friendly. Mr Peel realised, with startling clarity, that whatever he faced now he must face it clothed.

"Take off your clothes," he said to the writhing figure at his feet.

"What you saying?" Whined a horrified Kenny, who was now more afraid for his dignity than for his life. What respect could he ever hope for if this man left him naked? His fighting instinct kicked in and he leaped to his feat – but the pain in his ball struck him like lightening and he cried out.

Mr Peel lunged at him and grasped his dark blue top, pulling it over the boy's head before he could protest. In a flash Mr Peel had slipped it on. Though tight it felt almost luxurious next to his skin.

"Now the bottoms," he barked in his most authoritative voice. Kenny saw his friends standing warily in a loose semi-circle about three hundred yards off.

"Come on then!" he shouted plaintively to his friends. "Fucking help us!" He was starting to sulk. What was the point of being in a gang if they let you be publicly stripped by escapees from asylums? He decided to emphasise his humiliation rather than attempt to resist it. He sat on the ground and petulantly kicked off his tracksuit bottoms, revealing a long bright red pair of shorts beneath.

"You happy now?' he shouted – not at Mr Peel but at his friends. Mr Peel pulled on the too-tight tracksuit bottoms and put the cheque into the pocket.

Kenny's friends had, on the whole, only just risen from bed after a night sprinkled with small drug deals, one fight, two wild parties, and a chase by a much bigger and older gang through Brixton, Camberwell, and back again to their home turf of Kennington. There they had withdrawn to a flat on the estate and smoked a powerful strain of skunk weed called Cheese while watching videos.

Come morning the marijuana had left them feeling listless and crapulent and it was not until they saw the flash of Kenny's crimson shorts – part of their uniform – that they woke up to the fact that something very bad indeed was going on. Public humiliation of a blood was unthinkable.

"Let's fuck him up," said one and they began to close on Mr Peel.

Mr Peel saw their transformation - the muttered comment, the collective nod, the purposeful movement. He was about to engage, he reflected, in unarmed close combat with eight young black men. He could not win. When he saw the flash of a butterfly knife he decided to flee. He moved swiftly to Kenny's bike.

In the normal course of events Mr Peel would not have been able to ride Kenny's BMX at all. He would have scorned it as an instrument of torture or something belonging in a circus – but the fear of death can confer a sort of instant genius on a man and Mr Peel quickly found himself standing almost upright on the pedals with his feet rotating in a blur. He passed swiftly out of running range of the gang, which stopped and held a brief conference by the chain link fence. Should they get their bikes and give chase? The matter was decided when it was noticed that a group of girls had been watching the whole episode from a high window. Their laughter echoed around the estate – surely a taste of the mockery that would haunt their every move if they did not revenge this infamy. Like RAF pilots alerted to a Luftwaffe raid they scattered for their craft.

On exiting the park Mr Peel took a moment to get his bearings. Kennington was not, at that time, a particularly desirable part of London, but it is very close to the centre of town and Mr Peel recognised, with great relief, the stretch of road he was on. It leads directly towards Westminster Bridge – and once he crossed that he had only to go down Parliament Street and he was practically in The

Strand. And on the Strand, as he well knew, there was a NatWest Bank.

When Deputy Chief Inspector John Belton was handed the responsibility of policing the "Henry Espadrille/Trafalgar Square situation", he was well aware that he was looking (as he put it to his anxious wife Linda) "Down the barrel of a poisoned chalice." It was a time before social media, when the phenomenon of the 'flash mob' was not even a glint in the eye of the most computer literate techno geek on the planet, but DCI Belton had several reasons to believe that there would be a large gathering in Trafalgar Square to witness the appearance (in the unlikely event that it should actually occur) of the renegade Henry Espadrille. It was a crisp clear day after what seemed like weeks of rain, the kind of day when people felt a strong inclination to get out and about. The story had been running on BBC news bulletins through the morning with each report taking the trouble to include Henry Espadrille's on-stage announcement that he intended to hand himself into the authorities at noon. The independent channels had caught up at about 11 a.m., making up for their lack of footage from the talent night with lurid interviews with audience members as well as footage of an angry woman, apparently the partner of the talent night organiser, shouting at the press from an upstairs window of a house in Kennington. The print media, in their infinite stupidity, had also announced to the world that Mr Espadrille planned to hand himself over to the authorities at noon and their jaunty prose and insistence on splashing blown-up photographs of Mr Espadrille grinning happily on their covers seemed to suggest that what was expected was not a dangerous mentally ill man suspected of murder but an *al fresco* performance by an up and coming comedian. In fact some police intelligence had been trickling in that suggested quite a large crowd might gather. An undercover informant, who had infiltrated South Bank Polytechnic to try and find out who was supplying the students with ecstasy tablets, had told his handler that a group of art students planned to turn Espadrille's appearance into a bit of a 'happening' for 'ironic' reasons (whatever that meant). Meanwhile the press, in all their forms, were bound to be there. DCI Belton knew for a fact that most of the Sunday papers were holding their front pages.

His strategy had already been thrashed out with his deputies. Each of the roads leading into Trafalgar Square would be patrolled by one pair of officers on foot. If Mr Espadrille managed to evade them and enter the square then those officers would close in on him in a pincer movement. His immediate concern, which came into sharp relief in the cold light of dawn, was that these officers needed to operate in pairs in order to make a clean arrest (Henry Espadrille was quite a large man). They could not be on both sides of those streets at once. He would double the guard.

Should they fail to arrest Mr Espadrille before he entered the square he would be faced with the prospect of arresting him in front of a large and unpredictable audience. Might they get it into their heads that some sort of injustice was occurring? He intended to control the operation from a van parked in front of Admiralty Arch. A police van with eight officers in it would sit on the pedestrian area in front of the National Gallery, this unit to be deployed as and when they were needed. But it was clear now that he needed, at a discreet distance, and not visible to the public, a brigade of riot police and six mounted officers as well as a helicopter covering the entire operation.

There had been some difficulty in procuring all this extra capability at such short notice and the words "budgetary considerations" had been bandied about but he had finally pulled rank by calling the Chief Constable and explaining his predicament. They had attended Hendon Police College together and his old friend understood at once that there were all the ingredients here for a giant, and very public, cock up. He approved the requests but pointed out that if he fouled up the arrest he would probably not be able to save his bacon.

DCI Belton got to the square by 10.30 a.m. and was seated in the van by Admiralty Arch when the news came through that Henry Espadrille had been seen cycling naked through a council estate in Kennington. His felt a shudder of cold terror that began at his coccyx and fanned up to his shoulders – but he quickly calmed himself. With the reinforcements he had requested he now had the situation well in hand – and a naked cyclist, however extravagantly insane, was a vulnerable sort of creature. A new description of Mr Espadrille was issued.

It did not take Kenny's gang long to get mounted and mobile but they lost valuable time trying to guess in what direction their "disrespecter" had scarpered. Initially their instincts told them that he would have headed south – as they generally did themselves in a crisis – away from the higher concentration of authority found in the centre of town. But a chance encounter with one of their older brothers, passing the other way in a souped-up Corvette, provided them with the information that a 'Freaky looking brother in a too-small tracky-suit' was heading into town on a BMX. The gang moved off in swift unison.

They were just starting to give up hope of finding him when they clocked Mr Peel crossing Westminster Bridge in the far distance and their pursuit took on a renewed vigour. They caught up with him in Whitehall – but their euphoria was quickly replaced by paranoia as they noticed that police, their natural enemies, were everywhere. They passed a large van, as full as an egg with what looked like riot police, parked by the Cenotaph and there were beat coppers on both sides of the street. There was even a police chopper buzzing above them like a huge wasp. Although they were soon clustered tightly around Mr Peel, they were forced to accept that this was an inauspicious moment to chop him into small pieces. Instead they wreathed their faces in sinister grins while uttering promises to "kebab him." Until they could divert him into a side street they would have to be content with scaring him half to death.

DCI Belton had only just got used to the idea that a single night in London had reduced the dandyish Henry Espadrille to a state of cycling nudity, in his wildest imaginings he could not have guessed that within half an hour he had undergone another transformation – and become one of the nine hooded street gang members steaming up Parliament Street on their BMX stunt bikes. Consequently he gave orders for this little posse, albeit of highly suspicious looking characters, to be left unmolested. The last thing he wanted was accusations of heavy handed 'racial profiling' on a day when so many eyes were on his policing. In fact there was already a substantial number of people gathered in Trafalgar Square and DCI Belton assumed that the mounted street gang were intending to join them.

The crowd in the square consisted largely of what DCI Belton termed 'silly people' – the majority of whom were students with too few essays to write. He knew the type well - they were people for whom life was one endless extended joke. One group had turned up wearing Henry Espadrille masks – he presumed they were the art students from South Bank Polytechnic. The masks came courtesy of a newspaper (The Daily Sport), which had decided that it would be hilarious to provide a life size cut out of Henry Espadrille's face so that "You too can be someone else for a day." This little troupe of self-styled 'performance artists' had been entertaining the crowd since 10 a.m. by singing '"Underneath the Mango Tree"' while re-enacting what was apparently Mr Espadrille's signature dance. This had all made DCI Belton wince as he knew for a fact that Mrs Peel was in the square with her son Bill. He had been informed of this fact by a sharp-eyed constable and it pained him to think that she might have to witness people deriving merriment from her likely bereavement. He had to suppress a desire to order a great deal of old-fashioned truncheon work. Instead he deployed a couple of WPCs to go and check on Mrs Peel and her son.

In truth the crowd was a very disparate mix of people, ranging from lovers of true crime mysteries to comedy aficionados who were convinced that Henry Espadrille was a brilliant new character act who had drummed up a fake missing person narrative to hook in his audience. Of course once the crowd had reached about two hundred individuals its gravitational pull began to suck in tourists and passers by as well.

Mr Peel was not enjoying his progress up Parliament Street. The initial adrenaline surge had receded and he was now aware of the painful stiffening of muscles in his legs. The gang were terrifying him with their quietly uttered threats and he had just remembered that his route was going to take him past Trafalgar Square – the place where he had promised to turn himself in. It was likely that there would be police waiting for him. Although arrest now would save him from being cut to ribbons with butterfly knives the prospect of being captured when he was so near to the NatWest on the Strand was deeply dispiriting. He too had seen the van at the Cenotaph and the high number of police on the street but he had assumed this to be connected with some other event, perhaps a great matter of state or a political protest. When he arrived in the square he was initially lucky with the lights and was able to speed North towards the National Gallery with his murderous entourage still huddled about him, but they then hit stationary traffic and Mr Peel decided to mount the pavement. The crowd, bored by the performances of "Underneath the Mango Tree", turned its attention to the uniformed gang of young black youths on their comical little bikes.

Ironically Mr Peel's malevolent companions acted as an effective disguise and he was not recognised. He had pulled up his hood and the crowd, including the police amongst it, simply saw them as "a black street gang" and made little effort to distinguish individual faces. Even the detail of Mr Peel's bare feet, and the fact that his hoodie and tracksuit bottoms were ridiculously tight, failed to stand out. The gang itself glanced back at the mob as they rushed past, concluding that this was clearly some white people's protest, which bore no relevance to them. Their main interest was in the police, for whom they collectively put on their most innocent face. Only the brightest spark amongst them (their natural leader who was a chubby 14 year old called Tobin) noticed the Henry Espadrille masks and spotted their resemblance to their unwilling companion, but he did not immediately make sense of this.

Mr Peel was experiencing powerful emotions. Just before he had mounted the pavement he had spotted the figures of Caroline and Bill standing atop the steps around Nelson's column with two women police officers. Despite the cheerful crowd they looked dejected and sad and Mr Peel's heart contracted in pity for both them and himself. They represented everything that had fallen hopelessly beyond his reach – home, love, comfort - above all life without the imminent threat of a bloody death in a side alley.

With relief Mr Peel steered his bicycle off the pavement and back onto the road. He quickly crossed the North part of the square and shot into Duncannon Street, his accompanying pack of hoodies following effortlessly in his wake. They were close now to the NatWest Bank and Mr Peel had a sense that he could expend the last of his physical resources. He shot into the Strand, ignoring traffic and the shooting pains in his legs. He managed to put some space between himself and the gang but they quickly caught up with him, the whole group now swiftly slaloming through buses, taxis and other vehicles. When Mr Peel came abreast of the bank, which was on the other side of the street, he jumped off his bike and abandoned it. It clattered to the ground and two members of the gang crashed into it and tumbled off. This prompted a cacophony of screeching tyres and alarmed horn blasting and for a moment Mr Peel's pursuers were flung into disarray. But they quickly reformed and the two who had fallen leaped back on their bikes (one of them retrieved Kenny's bike and lead it off like a spare horse). They all flitted across to the pavement on the other side of the road, just in time to see Mr Peel walk stiffly into the bank. Not having legitimate business inside, and being well aware that entering on mass was likely to stir up trouble, the gang waited outside.

****

Daniel Bridger was disgustingly hung over and would have paid a month's salary not to have been working behind the till in NatWest on that particular Saturday morning. The night before had begun with a few pints with his mate Greg at the New Inn in North Wembley but at ten o'clock they had been struck with a heady sense of invincibility and had gone clubbing in the West End. This had, as usual, ended with tequila shots and a great deal of rejection by overly made-up girls – followed by more tequila shots as medicine for the soul and finally a ruinously expensive mini cab ride home, complete with window vomiting.

But every other week he had to be part of the NatWest pledge to be the most 'useful' bank in the UK and here he was on a precious Saturday, fighting the urge to dry heave into the waste paper basket at his feet and desperately trying to cobble together a smile for the customers.

When he saw the notorious Henry Espadrille standing panting in the queue in his tight street clothes, a good foot and a half of naked shin and calf flesh visible above his bare feet, his attitude changed. He knew him instantly, as did any Londoner who read the Evening Standard or indeed any British person with any interest in what was happening in the world. He had read the latest reports in The Sun through blood shot eyes on the tube journey that morning. It even made perfect sense to him that Henry Espadrille had come to the bank. One of the recurring themes in the Espadrille saga was that he seemed to like hanging around NatWest banks - there had been sightings of him at branches in Islington and Brixton – and of course his appearance at nearby Trafalgar Square was expected that morning.

Now Daniel prayed that he would be the one to deal with this bizarre and famous figure. He perked up considerably and dealt swiftly with his customer. Clearly if he himself dealt with whatever lunatic request the man had, he would gain some notoriety himself. What a man needed, to make himself attractive to makeup-caked tarts in the West End, was the sheen of fame. Henry Espadrille was going to get him laid.

To his horror his window became free at the same moment as Linda's, his neighbouring cashier, and a robotic female voice ordered Mr Espadrille to "Cashier number two please," which was Linda's window. Daniel watched as the key to his getting his end away passed blithely in front of him. "Would you like to come to this window please sir?" he interjected forcefully, startling Mr Peel and baffling Linda who had not yet noticed the ill-clad black man.

Mr Peel changed direction and presented himself at Daniel's window. He had already filled out the paying-in slip and he felt confident. The truth was that paying money in was a great deal easier than taking it out. He smiled at the sickly youth behind the counter and pulled the cheque out of his tracksuit pocket.

Daniel was holding his breath. What could Mr Espadrille possibly think he could get out of a NatWest bank? He was seated behind a bulletproof window and had a button near his right hand that would turn the customer area into a sealed steel box. The other customers, it was true, would then be trapped with a raving madman but he, Daniel would be safe and shaggably famous.

"I'd like to pay in a cheque please," said Mr Peel and Daniel's nervous smile became fixed and even more unnatural.

"What did you say sir?" he replied.

Mr Peel leaned forward – was this ashen-faced specimen deaf?

"I'd like to pay in a cheque please," he said again – and he pushed both the paying in slip and the cheque through the horizontal slot.

Daniel had been prepared for anything – a knife, a gun, a request for some imagined injustice to be righted. What he had not been prepared for was legitimate bank business. He picked up the cheque and examined it with an expert eye. Coutts and Co. always commanded respect. The sum was quite large and the cheque was filled out correctly. Apart from the 'paid in by' section (which was empty) the paying in slip was also in good order. The cheque was destined for the account of Michael Peel – the missing man. He looked up at Mr Espadrille who was staring back at him and attempting to disguise his mounting anxiety.

"You haven't signed the 'paid in by' section" said Daniel and passed it back to Mr Peel, whose hand hovered over the piece of paper, the NatWest biro clenched nervously. He had every right to put 'Michael Peel' but that might lead to problems. He wrote 'Henry Espadrille" and handed it back.

Daniel looked at what had been written and felt defeated. He had expected to see the name of the missing man, but he was seeing instead the man who stood in front of him. The situation was slipping out of his grasp. Could he expect to get his leg over some self-satisfied bint from Chorleywood if he simply conducted a legitimate bank transaction and sent Henry Espadrille on his way?

"Do you have any proof of identity?" he asked and Mr Peel took a deep breath. This was crunch time.

"What I am asking you to do is pay a Coutts and Company cheque made out to Michael Peel into the account of Michael Peel. I have paid in cheques a million times while wearing a smart suit and have never been asked to prove my identity. Perhaps what makes you suspect me of some evil intent is the combination of my clothing and the colour of my skin? "

Beside Daniel, Linda had stopped serving her customer as she picked up the forceful tone of the man at the next window. But when she saw him and heard what he was saying she felt, instinctively, that Daniel was probably being a twat. Daniel looked back at her and found that she was looking at him with her eyebrows raised in expectation. "Surely," continued Mr Peel, pressing his advantage, "any personal prejudices you hold against racial minorities have no place in a high street bank?"

Daniel felt that the situation was rapidly spiralling out of his control. Rather than emerging as a pussy magnet he was in danger of coming out of all this as an infamous bigot. He processed the cheque and confirmed that the money was now showing on Michael Peel's balance.

Out on the street the gang had became bored of waiting. Three of them had realised they were thirsty and they went into a shop a few doors down and there they came across the morning's newspapers – all showing the face of Henry Espadrille. Their leader Tobin bought a copy of *The Sun* and voraciously read the reports while the other two craned their necks and read the more sensational details out loud.

Mr Peel approached the exit door of the NatWest with trepidation. He could wait here in the bank until he was arrested – he had no further business out in the world now that the cheque was banked – but he longed to speak to Caroline and Bill. If he didn't speak to them now he might not see them until he was on trial for his own murder. He could see the gang of black youths waiting for him through the glass door and the thought of handing himself over to their custody was not pleasant. He turned to look back at the dreary interior of the bank. The dry stale air was oppressive. Despite his exhaustion, the terrible stiffness in his legs, and the sense that he was in a place of safety, the idea of staying there until he was arrested depressed him. His wife and son were just a few hundred yards away and he had to at least try and reach them. They were hardly going to visit a strange black man in police custody – especially one who was accused of killing Michael Peel. The gang could do little in broad daylight on the Strand – and he would soon be in the safe custody of the law.

He stepped out onto the street to find the gang ranged in a semi-circle on their bikes.

Mr Peel glanced at them briefly, his expression inviting them to do their worst, then began to walk purposefully along the pavement towards Trafalgar Square.

They followed him, circling him on the pavement on their bikes.

"Did you know you was in the papers?" asked Tobin, as he casually performed a minor stunt that employed the curb.

"I guessed as much," replied Mr Peel – who was peering towards Nelson's column and calculating what his chances were of reaching Caroline and Bill.

"Did you murder that white man then?" asked another, the tinge of respect in his voice striking Mr Peel as frankly sinister.

"There are a great deal of policemen around, I don't know if you noticed,' countered Mr Peel.

"So what?" said Tobin "We done nothing wrong – you is the criminal."

"You is wearing stolen threads too – Kenny's threads," chirped another.

"I'm sorry about your friends clothes – it was unforgivable," said Mr Peel.

"It was disrespectful," said Tobin – a comment that received vigorous assent from the others.

"It was an act of desperation," said Mr Peel. "Look I'll tell you what – when I'm out of jail or wherever they put me – you must all come to lunch in my house in Kent."

This produced an abrupt burst of laughter, which utterly confused Mr Peel. Was an invitation to lunch a joke these days?

"You really thinks you is that white geezer don't you?" said Tobin, with the smile of a young man talking to a lunatic.

Mr Peel sighed, they had nearly reached the square where, he was pretty certain, there was going to be an ugly scene. He did not want to involve these young people, uncouth and over-fond of knives though they were.

"Look I'm definitely going to be arrested now," he said. "I apologise about Kenny's tracksuit – but you've got nothing to gain by associating with me now. It might well lead to you all being arrested as well – and I don't suppose you want that."

"Maybe we do," said Tobin.

"Maybe we don't care one ways or the other," added the one who happened to be passing in front of Mr Peel at that moment, the spare bike being lead expertly by his free hand. "Maybe we gots nothing to lose." He continued as he passed behind Mr Peel's back to be quickly replaced by another.

The truth was that Henry Espadrille had excited in them a complex set of emotions. As a human being he struck them as about the most vulnerable creature they had ever encountered. His outrageous delusion of whiteness combined with his posh accent would have exposed him to violent ridicule on the estate – yet despite these provocations he had entered their lives as naked as a babe. Whether this was prompted by courage or insanity they could not tell. But combined with the fact that he was wanted for a serious crime, that he was trying to speak to his wife and child and that Trafalgar Square seemed to be heaving with police – the result was a complete transformation in their attitude towards Henry Espadrille. Despite the fact that he had exposed Kenny's scarlet underpants to giggling girls they now felt a primeval urge to protect him.

"We's gonna hep you," Tobin announced simply, and his underlings ceased circling Mr Peel and cycled instead in the same direction he was walking. "You're just one of us right? Just another black kid innit."

Mr Peel was touched to find that his erstwhile pursuers had transformed into loyal allies but he was unsure what use to make of them. They were now approaching the pedestrian crossing at the bottom of the Strand and could see the milling crowd in Trafalgar Square and its accompanying police presence.

"My wife and son are on the steps of Nelson's column," said Mr Peel. "Maybe you could get me to the steps – so I can speak to them before I'm arrested."

Tobin braked and made a hand gesture that formed his troop into a huddle. Mr Peel heard only a muttering and the words "Use the bikes innit," then they broke up.

"We'll get you there," said Tobin, proffering the spare bike. Mr Peel looked with distaste at the little bicycle – amazed now that he had even managed to sit on it, let alone ride it all the way from Kennington. The fear of a knife in the guts, he reflected, had proved a powerful incentive.

"I really don't think I can ride that thing another inch," he said, but Tobin wasn't satisfied. He made a sort of squelching sound with his mouth while looking at one of his companions, who turned out to be the chief engineer. He dismounted his own bike and whipped out a multi-tool. Within seconds he had extended the saddle on Kenny's bike to its full height.

They steered onto the road and crossed it during a wide gap in the traffic. Mr Peel began to feel more comfortable and they gathered speed – but he had forgotten to put up his hood and he was almost immediately recognised by one of the policemen stationed at the corner of Parliament Street, who radioed the news through to DCI Belton.

In his van DCI Belton barked out the order for all units to close on the suspect who was approaching the square at the West end of the Strand with a gang of black youths on BMX bikes. The four policemen on the Strand broke into a run but although they quickly caught up with the huddle of cyclists the boys were so closely bunched together that it proved impossible to distinguish which one was Henry Espadrille, and the group was accelerating fast. They shot across a pedestrian crossing, ignoring the red light completely, causing an SUV to halt suddenly. A taxi rammed into its back and a second car rammed into that. The crowd had only just turned their attention to this traffic accident when they became aware that

Policemen were running into the square from all sides and the huddle of bike-mounted hoodies was riding straight towards the throng of people around Nelson's column. The crowd opened up to let them through.

Mr Peel was now doubly protected, both by the crowd and his praetorian guard. Realizing this, DCI Belton yelled unprofessionally into his radio, ordering the riot police into the square with instructions to open up a route into the crowd so that Espadrille could be plucked out. When these men, in their black suits of armour and riot shields, entered the square at a steady trot the crowd, which had woken up to the fact that their new hero was the tall figure at the heart of the gang, was instantly gripped by the collective certainty that Henry Espadrille was innocent and must be protected.

Mrs Peel and her son Bill had been about to give up waiting for Mr Peel's abductor to make an appearance and go for a coffee in the National Gallery café when the BMX gang appeared, followed swiftly by the troop of riot police. Mrs Peel knew at once that Henry Espadrille was trying to get to where she stood on the steps of Nelson's column because he had looked directly at her as he barrelled into the crowd on his strange little bike. She steeled herself for the coming encounter. The two policewomen tried to persuade her to step around to the other side of the column but she firmly held her ground. "I'm going to give him a piece of my mind," she insisted. Bill, seeing his mother's determination, advised them that she was not going to be persuaded otherwise.

DCI Belton had clambered out of the van. The helicopter footage that he was watching on his monitor of the writhing mob at the centre of Trafalgar Square was hopelessly confused. Not only was it impossible to distinguish which of the cyclists was Espadrille but he could not even make out who his own forces were in the general melee. He announced to his deputy that he was going to "take the fucker myself" and his deputy nodded sagely as he observed the last panicked flailings of a man about to be relieved of high office. Still clutching his radio DCI Belton ran across the road and flung himself into the crowd. Ahead of him he saw that Henry Espadrille had almost reached Mrs Peel, who stood like some incarnation of Britannia, staring steadily out across the English Channel and preparing to defend herself against an invader.

"He's going to attack that woman!" shouted DCI Belton – and the crowd seemed to suddenly suffer a crisis of identity. Had they been wrong all along about this Espadrille character? Was he in fact a dangerous lunatic? At this moment the first of the riot policemen reached the dark ring of hoodies around Mr Peel. Tobin shouted "now" and they all dismounted, lifting their bikes up onto their shoulders, so that the bike wheels acted like shields. They then joined hands through the gaps between spokes creating a fortified sanctuary. Mr Peel was as surprised as anyone by this turn of events but he quickly realised that they had won him a few precious moments. The riot police were forced to grapple with spokes and tyres in an effort to open a gap in the ring of steel around their suspect – forcing them into an undignified tug of war with their opponents.

"Caroline!" called out Mr Peel. "Caroline listen to me."

DCI Belton had now reached the circle of BMX shields. "Henry Espadrille," he yelled as he furiously tried to pry open a gap between two bikes, "I am arresting you in connection with the disappearance of Michael Peel." This produced a laugh from the crowd who, though unable to see exactly what was happening, could see clearly that Henry Espadrille was not in anyone's custody. In fact, having ditched his bike, he was standing completely unmolested at the centre of the writhing circle of struggling men and bicycles.

Mrs Peel took a deep breath and looked Henry Espadrille in the eye.

"How dare you," she bellowed, "come uninvited into my home." Her voice was so strident it silenced the crowd and had the affect of freezing the movements of the riot police. Beside her Bill was suffering agonies of embarrassment at the public spectacle his mother was making of herself. He plunged his hands into his pockets and felt a cold glass object.

"An Englishman's home is his castle!" pronounced Mrs Peel, her fury mounting, "and what you did stamped on that sacred law. I don't care what colour you are or what form of mental frailty you use as an excuse for your actions – you have offended me and I demand an apology. An apology and an answer to one simple question: Where is my husband? What have you done with Michael?" This question raised a cheer from the crowd who knew whose side they were on now. It was the fine old posh lady on the steps – a living symbol of English grit and pride.

The gang not only sensed the shift in the allegiance of the crowd but also noticed that the lady standing shouting on the steps was white. In addition the man standing beside her was also white and could not be any natural son of the dark-skinned Mr Espadrille. They had been tricked into assisting a nutcase.

They let the riot police through and they all fell on Mr Peel, quickly entwining him in their arms like a powerful dark blue octopus gripping its evening meal. DCI Belton managed to get his arm around Mr Peel's neck.

"I am Michael Peel!" He managed to roar – and before a chorus of boos could overwhelm him he managed to add, "And I'll prove it to you here and now."

On the steps Bill took the mysterious glass object out of his pocket and examined it. It was the little jar in which, the day before, he had placed the moth he caught on the kitchen windowsill.

"Ask me any question Caroline," gasped Mr Peel through DCI Belton's tight neck hold, "before these witnesses – ask me a question about our life – something a stranger could not possibly know – and I'll answer it."

DCI Belton did not like this development. A confidence trickster was taking command of the mob. He knew very well that such characters were capable of pulling off the most astonishing *coups de theatre* before gullible crowds.

"That's enough of that," he shouted. "Come on lads let's get him out of here." He gestured with his free arm for those police not gripping a part of Mr Peel's anatomy to open up a channel through the crowd, but although they began to do this, the crowd immediately fought back by pressing in on the huddle of arresting officers, refusing to be robbed of a satisfying denouement to the drama.

"Go on ask him!" someone shouted and "Ask him, ask him, ask him…" became the repeated chant of the crowd - delivered with an aggressive edge. The situation was getting ugly. DCI Belton saw someone being bonked on the head with a truncheon and heard a sickly thud followed by an unhealthy yelp. It was one of the people in a Henry Espadrille mask and the sight of him going down struck

DCI Belton as particularly grotesque. He decided to take another tack.

"Alright one question!" he roared – and he gestured to his men for calm. "One question and then will you allow us to undertake our public duty and arrest a man wanted in connection with a missing person?" The crowd concurred and all eyes turned on Caroline Peel.

But what could she ask him? It had to be something secret – that only she and Michael knew, but in this great public place, with all these eyes on her – the idea of thinking of such a thing, let alone sharing it, seemed utterly remote. Beside her Bill opened the little jar and peeped inside. At the bottom was a neat little grey moth, its wings folded into a triangle, waiting for its circumstances to improve with infinite patience.

Mrs Peel had it – the desert rose! The flower on their honeymoon. This was their great secret and if someone had told her, a day before, that she would one day raise the issue in front of hundreds of strangers she would have laughed at them. But perhaps, after all, there was some logic to this – perhaps the secret had a purpose. It was there to expose this villain and properly start the process whereby he would be forced to reveal where he had hidden Michael before being placed inside a steel cage for his remaining days.

"Alright!" she shouted. "Tell me this – on our honeymoon my husband bought a flower. It was on my pillow on the first night in the hotel. If you really are Michael you'll be able to tell me - what flower was it?"

The romantic nature of this question pleased almost everyone in the crowd, even some of the hardened riot police. In fact there was a collective sigh followed by only a small collective laugh from the cynical and permanently amused. But the effect of the question on Mr Peel was devastation. The truth was (and he suddenly felt the awful shame of this) he had never bought Caroline flowers in his life. It was something he just found too awkward - too un-English. Whenever the impulse had possessed him in the past he had suddenly felt stiff and absurd – like a grey-suited accountant faced with the prospect of performing a pirouette. He had the faintest memory of something pink being left on the bed on the honeymoon, and how it had cheered her up no end, but the one thing that was beyond all doubt was that it had bugger all to do with him.

"I didn't buy any bloody flower!" he yelled. He had not intended to swear but his despair gave way to anger as he spoke. What was this obsession with dead plants?

The crowd now turned against Henry Espadrille. They had gone from wanting to protect him to wanting to hear what he had to say. Now, though, they wanted to punish him. He had sworn at this fine woman, revealed himself to be an impostor, and, in the same breath, shown himself to be brutally unromantic. The men holding him started squeezing him and others nearby began throwing punches. DCI Belton realised that this was now a rescue operation.

Mr Peel continued shouting towards Mrs Peel but she caught only some of his words. "I've never bought you flowers in my life," he yelled before a punch caught him on the right cheek. The truth of this statement did not improve her mood although it had to be admitted that, saving that single desert rose, this was actually true of her real husband.

Bill had by now retreated into a little world of his own. If you are going to lose your father, he was reflecting, this was surely the least dignified and most traumatic way you could do it; with a lunatic black man, claiming to be your dad and writhing like a great fish in the midst of an infuriated mob. He looked at the moth at the bottom of the jar. In all this craziness, on this sad day when he should perhaps accept that his father was gone for good, it would be a fitting tribute if he released this poor creature. Bill had no idea what moth it was, although its distinctive squat triangle shape and speckled markings triggered some vague memory. His father, of course, would have known it immediately. He poked his finger into the jar and the moth took flight.

The small grey creature soared sharply upwards flapping its wings in wild relief at its sudden freedom. The cold jar with its featureless walls had been a hideous prison. The frantic beating of its wings quickly brought it high above the square where, momentarily, it came eye-to-eye with the sandstone Lord Nelson atop his column. There a pigeon swooped momentarily in front of the winter sun and the moth's heart was gripped with terror. Below there was a thick press of policemen around Mr Peel who was almost having the breath squeezed out of him by the pressing mob. Half the crowd seemed to be determined to get at least one punch in to assuage their feelings of outrage.

The swooping pigeon having focused the moth's tiny mind, it headed sharply downwards, mistaking the swirling shapes below it for windblown undergrowth. It finally alighted on a policeman's helmet right in front of Mr Peel's face. Even in his extremely straightened circumstances, with men trying to arrest him, others trying to assault him and at least two attempting to grab his clothes as souvenirs, Mr Peel was enchanted to see a peppered moth – a fine specimen with the characteristic darker markings that made it such a favourite of secondary school teachers tasked with explaining evolution. The shared experience of altered pigmentation, though experienced by the moth in a very different way to his own, was not lost on Mr Peel. His eyes lit up and he spontaneously shouted for his son.

"Bill!" he roared. It was a joyous roar and Bill picked up on its timbre immediately. "Bill come here," he shouted again and he sought out his son's eyes above the crowd on the steps. Bill simply could not resist the innocent note of fatherly excitement in the voice – his own father's voice – and he started forcibly working his way towards Henry Espadrille. "Bill look – look," cried Mr Peel. "It's my associate - a peppered moth – my fellow – it's the most curious thing."

Bill stared wide eyed at the moth which, miraculously, remained on the jerking helmet of the policeman, who was engaged in a slow motion struggle with an engineering student from Leith.

"It's the one I caught in the kitchen yesterday," exclaimed Bill and he looked at Henry Espadrille - but the man who looked back at him performed a facial expression, a raising of the eyebrows with a happy glint in the eye – which could only be his father's. This was not Henry Espadrille – this was his dad, and his dad was being torn apart by the mob.

He turned back to the steps, "Mum!" He shouted desperately. "Mum – it's him – it's Dad!"

Mrs Peel met her son's eyes and saw at once his absolute certainty. A whole series of pieces slotted into place in her mind; the fact that he had been seated on the side of the bed on that fateful morning just as Michael did, with his feet at a funny angle, Aunt Alice being convinced by his voice, his knowing, just now, that he never bought flowers, the characteristic swearing, and again that voice! What had she been thinking?

By now Mr Peel was being held aloft like a corpse in an effort by the police to protect him from the mob.

"It's my father!" Bill started shouting at anyone who would listen. "Michael Peel is not missing!" He now saw, standing close to him, the figure of DCI Belton with his distinctive uniform. Bill at once recognised him as the figure of ultimate authority in the square and he grabbed him by the lapels.

DCI Belton did not like being grabbed in this way but he did not have the free use of his arms, which were pinned to his sides by the increasingly alarming crush. "We're dropping all charges," Bill was shouting in his face, "we've found Michael Peel". These shouts made no sense to DCI Belton who, in any case, was far too busy trying to free his right arm so that he could raise his radio to his mouth and order the mounted police to enter the fray. He knew, for certain, that he was going to be spending a great deal of time playing golf from now on, and it had to be said that the thought was not entirely unwelcome – but his last duty was to order the horses in. If there was one thing that terrified an urban rabble it was the astonishing sight of these beautiful creatures bearing down on them. After a brief and superhuman struggle he managed to issue the order.

****

The effect of the six mounted officers on their fine steeds was very much as might be predicted. The crowd began to disperse as quickly as it could, with only the hardest student anarchists feeling that only by smashing a plate glass window or two could they fully communicate their feelings about the Henry Espadrille saga. In fact within half an hour a good proportion of the rabble was enjoying the educational benefits of a visit either to the National Gallery or the National Portrait Gallery, where they tried to look studious and respectable. After an hour a couple of crumpled coffee cups, the odd dropped glove, a Nike trainer and a few tattered Henry Espadrille masks were the only signs that there had been a minor riot in Trafalgar Square.

The media had indeed captured a great little picture story. The photograph that would be most favoured by editors showed Henry Espadrille being gripped by the tightly packed and heavily police-tinged crowd. The picture was taken by a media savvy Japanese tourist from the top of an open topped sightseeing bus, and it had the ironic effect of making Mr Espadrille seem like a revered icon being carried in a religious procession.

In fact after the crowd had melted away and DCI Belton had managed to make his arrest he was disappointed to discover that the cause of all the trouble, Henry Espadrille, was in need of first aid. What is more Mrs Peel and her son seemed to have become inordinately fond of him and insisted on clinging to his side. It was agreed that they would all walk over to an ambulance that was now parked next to his control van in front of Admiralty Arch and while Henry Espadrille's thumb was being bandaged and a black eye treated with iodine the situation became, for DCI Belton, even more bizarre and infuriating.

In the ambulance Mrs Peel sat beside her husband clutching his arm and Bill stood at the open doors. The senior policeman sat opposite Mr and Mrs Peel, holding his hand to his forehead as he tried desperately to understand what was going on.

"We're just going to take him home if that's alright,' repeated Mrs Peel, who had received no answer when she first uttered these words.

"It's been a misunderstanding," continued Bill. "This was Michael Peel all along."

"I'm sorry but I can't accept that," said DCI Belton, in his most authoritative voice.

" It is Michael," affirmed Mrs Peel. "This is my husband – we've been married for forty-two years so – if you'll excuse me for insisting – I think I'd know."

"But..." spluttered DCI Belton, grappling for the right words. "He's – look, I have seen pictures of Michael Peel – this is not him."

"I know my own husband," insisted Mrs Peel, a hint of the tigress creeping in to her voice.

"It's him – it's my father," said Bill, with great finality and Mr Peel winked at his son while grinning and giving him an affectionate pat on the arm with his free hand.

"But he's the wrong colour!" blurted DCI Belton, no longer able to contain himself – and immediately regretted it. The medic who was bandaging Mr Peel's painfully sprained thumb now stopped his work and turned to look, with some shock, at the senior policeman who had just uttered this nakedly racist remark. Being himself a third generation Ghanaian immigrant he felt his heart sink at the realisation that things in Britain had not really improved since his grandfather, Bernie, had been the victim of police brutality in Brixton in 1978.

"What do you mean the wrong colour?" asked Bill, leaning into the ambulance and fixing DCI Belton with a confident stare. "How can a man be the wrong colour? If you have personal prejudices about skin colour – surely you should keep them to yourself?"

"Now just a minute I didn't say..."

"You said he was the wrong colour – it was as clear as day."

"If you are prejudiced about these things," said Mrs Peel, reasonably, "you should really keep it under your hat – especially a man in your position."

"Look I am not saying he is the wrong colour. I am saying he is not Michael Peel – I know Michael Peel..."

"I don't think I've met you before," said Mr Peel, politely, as though talking to someone at a drinks party.

"I didn't say I've met you," said DCI Belton, now fighting to hold his temper "I've seen your picture in the papers."

"You shouldn't trust the British press," said Bill, "they're notoriously unreliable."

"Look – if I'm not Michael Peel my own family are going to cotton on to it pretty quick aren't they?" said Mr Peel. "I mean, when we got home I wont know where anything is, will I?"

"Well you don't know where anything is." said Mrs Peel, unhelpfully. She looked at DCI Belton. "You wouldn't believe what I have to put up with."

"Now come on that's not fair," said Mr Peel, genuinely aggrieved.

"You don't know where the cheese grater is kept do you?" his wife continued, getting into her stride. "I must have told you a thousand times – but you always ask – drives me to distraction." A smile had formed on Bill's face.

"I do know where the cheese grater is," said Mr Peel, calculating, correctly, that his wife wouldn't call him on this. "Really officer," protested Mr Peel, "she's making me out to be some sort of monster."

The little discussion continued a little longer but DCI Belton had in fact withdrawn from the fray. As soon as he observed the pair arguing like an old married couple he knew that his number was up. He was going to have to release the man here and now – and then explain even that to the Chief Constable, along with the entire fiasco in the square. But he was not feeling sad or defeated. In fact he felt in his breast an uncomplicated upsurge of love, not for humanity in general nor for Mr and Mrs Peel and their son in particular (nor, for that matter, for his wife Linda). The love he felt was for one very specific activity – namely the guiding of small white balls into small dark holes. He would play golf now, every chance he got, until he breathed his last - and he was OK with that.

He was however, still just engaged enough with the situation to try and acquire a bit of protective paper work. He asked the Peels if they would accompany him to nearby police station so that something could be typed up properly but Mrs Peel quickly detected that this was merely a request and it carried no legal force – he was not arresting anybody. In the end she wrote out, in long hand, a statement that "The man who previously claimed to be Henry

Espadrille is in fact my husband Michael Peel." She signed it and they bid DCI Belton goodbye.

The Peel family made their way across Trafalgar Square towards Charing Cross station and the 3.10 p.m. train to Tonbridge. The coming months would prove to be challenging – characterised by a great deal of tongue-wagging in their neighbourhood and a good deal of unnecessary visits by family, friends and acquaintances. These visits in their turn tended to feature prolonged bouts of astonished gaping-mouthed staring at Mr Peel and occasional explosive rows as he responded, as any reasonable man might, to the suggestion that he was not who he claimed to be. Gradually things settled down and, with the mortgage paid off and Mr Peel's pension starting to pay out, relatively decorous, semi-rural, comfortable, middle class, English normality prevailed.

###

Connect with the author on line:
Website: http://wordsontoast.weebly.com/
Facebook: http://www.facebook.com/thepepperedmoth
Twitter: @AdamPreston

Printed in Great Britain
by Amazon